BOSTON ILLUSTRATED.

BOSTON:
JAMES R. OSGOOD & Co.

Price 50 cents.

BOSTON ILLUSTRATED.

I. A GLANCE AT ITS HISTORY.

BOSTON was originally "by the Indians called Shawmutt," but the colonists of 1630, wandering southward from their landing-place at Salem, named it Trimountaine. Charlestown, which was occupied by them in July, 1630, was speedily abandoned because there was found no good spring of water, and the peninsula close by having been bought of its sole inhabitant, the settlement was transferred thither on the 7th of September, O. S. (17th N. S.). On the same day the court held at Charlestown ordered that Trimountaine be called Boston. This name was given to it in memory of Boston in Old England, from which many of the colonists had emigrated, and which was the former home of Mr. Isaac Johnson, next to Governor Winthrop the most important man among the band of emigrants. The name of Trimountaine, which has been transformed into Tremont, was peculiarly appropriate. As seen from Charlestown, the peninsula seemed to consist of three high hills, afterwards named Copp's, Beacon, and Fort. And the highest of the three was itself a trimountain, having three sharp little peaks. It seems to be agreed that this peculiarity of Beacon Hill was what gave to the place its ancient name.

MR. BLACKSTONE'S HOUSE.

The first settler in Boston was Mr. William Blaxton, or Blackstone, who had lived here several years when the Massachusetts Colony was formed. Soon after selling the land to the new company of immigrants, he withdrew to the place which now bears his name, the town of Blackstone, on the border of Rhode Island.

Boston was selected as the centre and metropolis of the Massachusetts Colony. The nucleus of the Colony was large, and the several towns lying along the coast were, under all the circumstances, rapidly settled. During the year 1630 as many as fifteen hundred persons came from England. In ten years not less than twenty thousand had been brought over. The records show that in 1639 there was a muster in Boston of the militia of the Colony to the number of a thousand able-bodied and well-armed men. It is impossible to learn accurately the population of Boston at any time during the first century after its settlement, since no enumeration was made; but there is authority for the statement that in 1674 there were about fifteen hundred families in the town, and the population of New England was then reckoned at one hundred and twenty thousand.

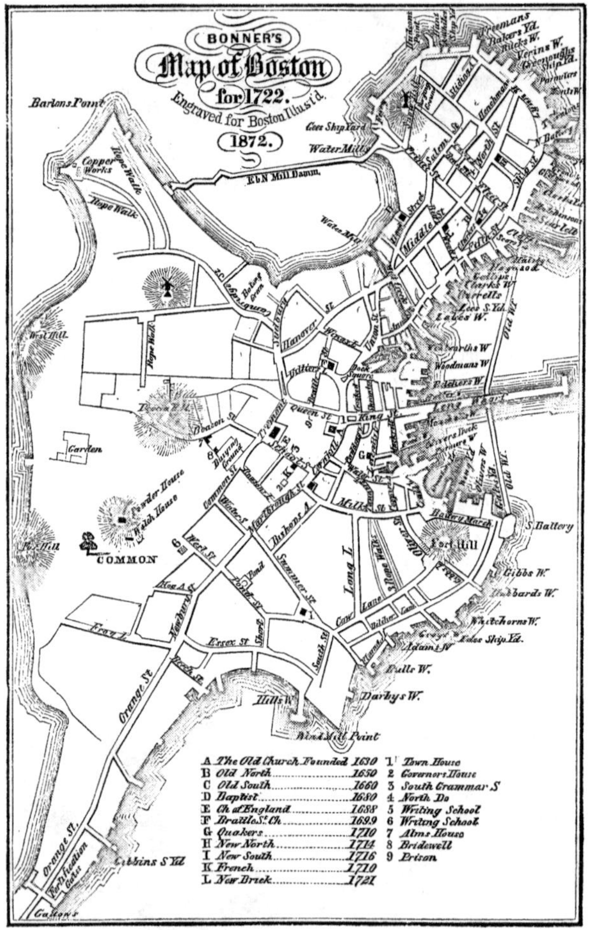

The early history of Boston has been an almost inexhaustible field for the researches of local antiquaries. Considering that almost three quarters of a century elapsed before the first newspaper was printed, the materials for making a complete account of the events that occurred, and for forming a correct estimate of the habits and mode of life of the people, are remarkably abundant. The records have been searched to good purpose. Still it is to visitors that we are indebted for some of the most quaint and interesting pictures of early New England life. An English traveller, named Edward Ward, published in London in 1699 an account of his trip to New England, in which he describes the customs of Bostonians in a lively manner, and perhaps with a degree of truthfulness, though some parts of the story are evidently exaggerated. Mr. Ward thought it a great hardship that "Kissing a Woman in Public, tho' offer'd as a Courteous Salutation," should be visited with the heavy punishment of whipping for both the offenders. There were even then "stately Edifices, some of which have cost the owners two or three Thousand Pounds sterling," and this fact Mr. Ward rather illogically conceived to prove the truth of two old adages, "That a Fool and his Money is soon parted; and, Set a Beggar on Horseback he 'll ride to the Devil; for the Fathers of these Men were Tinkers and Peddlers." He seemed to have a very low opinion of the religious and moral character of the people. Mr. Daniel Neal, who wrote a book a few years later, found "the conversation in this town as polite as in most of the cities and towns in England," and he describes the houses, furniture, tables, and dress as being quite as splendid and showy as those of the most considerable tradesmen in London.

But while we find such abundant means of judging the people of Boston, hardly a vestige of the town as it appeared to the earliest settlers remains. We have, it is true, in a good state of preservation still, the three most ancient burial-grounds of the town ; half a dozen very old trees remain ; about as many buildings. Some of the narrow and crooked streets at the North End have retained their early devious course, but generally appear upon the map under changed names. Nothing else of Boston in its first century is preserved. The face of the country has been completely transformed. The hills have been cut down, and the flats surrounding the peninsula have been filled so that it is a peninsula no longer. Place side by side a map of Boston as it appeared in 1722, and the latest map, and any resemblance between them can hardly be traced. The old water line has disappeared completely. On the east, the west, and the south, nearly a thousand acres once covered by the tide have been reclaimed, and are now covered with streets, dwellings, and warehouses.

It would be interesting to dwell upon the early history of Boston, and to discover indications of the gradual formation of the New England character, but all this curious study must be left to the historian. A few facts and dates only can find a place here. Boston was from the first a commercial town. Less than a year had elapsed since the settlement of the town when the first vessel built in the colony was launched. We may infer something in regard to the activity of the foreign and coasting trade from the statement of Mr. Neal, before referred to, that "the masts of ships here, and at proper seasons of the year, make a kind of wood of trees like that we see upon the river of *Thames* about *Wapping* and *Limehouse*" ; and the same author says that twenty-four thousand tons of shipping were at that time, 1719, cleared annually from the port of Boston. It was not until four years after the settlement of the town that a shop was erected separate from the dwelling of the proprietor. In these early days the merchants of Boston met with many reverses, and wealth was acquired but slowly in New England generally. Nevertheless, the town was on the whole prosperous. In 1741 there were forty vessels upon the stocks at one time in Boston, showing that a quick demand for shipping existed at that period. At the close of the seventeenth century, Boston was probably the largest and wealthiest town in America, and it has ever since retained its rank among the very first towns on the continent.

The colonists brought their minister with them, — the Rev. John Wilson, who was ordained pastor of the church in Charlestown, and afterwards of the church in Boston. But the meeting-house was not built until 1632. This building was very small and very plain, within and without. It is believed to have stood nearly on the spot where Brazer's Building now stands, near the Old State House, in State Street. In 1640 the same society occupied a new, much larger and finer building, which stood on the site now occupied by Joy's Building on Washington Street. This second edifice stood seventy-one years, and was destroyed by fire in 1711. The "First Church" removed a few years ago from Chauncy Street to its present very elegant church building on Berkeley Street. Several other churches were established very soon after the "First," and there are now in existence as many as nine church organizations dating back to the first hundred years after the place was settled. The fathers of the town were sternly religious, outwardly at all events. The evidences are abundant that they were also zealous for education. The influence of Harvard College, in Cambridge, was strong upon Boston from the first; but a public school had been voted by the town in 1635, three years before Harvard was founded. We have seen the testimony of an Englishman as to the polished manners, intelligence, and education of the inhabitants of Boston, and this evidence is confirmed by our own records and by the long line of eminent clergymen, writers, and orators born in the town.

FIRST CHURCH IN BOSTON.

It was here that the first newspaper ever published on the American continent, the "Boston News Letter," appeared on the 24th of April, 1704. Two years later the first great New England journalist, and afterwards a philosopher, statesman, and diplomatist, was born in a little house that stood near the head of Milk Street, and that is still remembered by some of the oldest citizens of Boston. It was destroyed by fire at the close of the year 1811, after having stood almost a hundred and twenty years.

BIRTHPLACE OF BENJAMIN FRANKLIN.

The history of the thirty years preceding the Revolution is full of incidents showing the independent spirit of the inhabitants of Boston, their determination not to submit to the unwarrantable interference of the British government in their affairs, and particularly to the unjust taxation imposed upon the Colonies, and their willingness to incur any risks rather than yield to oppression. As early as 1747 there was a great riot in Boston, caused by the aggression of British naval officers. Commodore Knowles, being short of men, had impressed sailors in the streets of Boston. The people made reprisals by seizing some British officers, and holding them as hostages for the return of their fellow-citizens. The excitement was very great, but the affair terminated by the release of the impressed men and the naval officers, the first victory registered to the account of the resisting colonists. Twenty years later the town was greatly agitated over the Stamp Act; and hardly had the excitement died away when, on March 5, 1770, the famous Boston Massacre took place. The story is familiar to every school-boy. The affair originated without any special grievance on either side, but the whole population took the part of the mob against the soldiers, showing what a deep-seated feeling of hostility existed even then. The scene of this massacre was the square in King Street, now State Street, below the Old State House. The well-known woodcut of the scene shows the State House in the background, but in a form quite different from the present. This building was erected in 1748, on the site occupied by the Town House destroyed by fire the year previous. It has long been given up to business purposes, the interior has been completely remodelled, and the edifice surmounted by a roof that has wholly destroyed the quaint effect of the original architecture. It was in its day, we are assured by history, "an elegant building." The accompanying picture shows the Old State House in its ancient form. How it appears to-day may be seen from the view on another page. The funeral of the victims of the massacre was attended by an immense concourse of people from all parts of New England, and the impression made by the conflict upon the patriotic men of that day did not die out until the war of the Revolution had begun. The day was celebrated for several years as a memorable anniversary. The newspapers of the day did their full share towards keeping up the excitement. The "Massachusetts Spy," which began publication in Boston in 1770, was one of the most earnest of the patriotic press, and two or three years before the beginning of the war had, at the head of its columns, an invocation to Liberty, with a coarse woodcut of a serpent cut into nine parts, attacked by a dragon. The several parts of the serpent were marked "N. E." for New England, "N. Y.," "N. J.," and so on, and above this cut was the motto "Join, or Die."

THE OLD STATE-HOUSE.

The destruction of the tea in Boston Harbor was another evidence of the spirit of the people. The ships having "the detested tea" on board arrived the last of November and the first of December, 1773. Having kept watch over the ships to prevent the landing of any of the tea until the 16th of December, and having failed to compel the consignees to send the cargoes back to England, the people were holding a meeting on the subject on the afternoon of the 16th, when a formal refusal by the Governor of a permit for the vessels to pass the castle without a regular custom-house clearance was received. The meeting broke up, and the whole assembly followed a party of thirty persons disguised as Indians to Griffin's (now Liverpool) Wharf, where the chests were broken open and their contents emptied into the dock. The secret of the participators in this affair has been well kept, and it is doubtful if any additional light will ever be thrown upon it. It has been claimed, though on very doubtful authority, that the plot was concocted in the quaint old building that stood until a few years since on the corner of Dock Square and North (formerly Ann) Street. This building was constructed of rough-cast in the year 1680, after the great fire of 1679; and was until 1860, when it was taken down, one of the most curious specimens of architecture in Boston. A cut of this old building is given, without any voucher of the tradition that assigns to a certain room in it the origin of a bold act that led to such momentous consequences.

OLD HOUSE IN DOCK SQUARE.

The people of the town took as prominent a part in the war when it broke out as they had taken in the preceding events. They suffered in their commerce and in their property by the enforcement of the Boston Port Act, and by the occupation of the town by British soldiers. Their churches and burial-grounds were desecrated by the English troops, and annoyances without number were put upon them, but they remained steadfast through all. General Washington took command of the American army July 2, 1775, in Cambridge, but for many months there was no favorable opportunity for making an attack on Boston. During the winter that followed, the people of Boston endured many hardships, but their deliverance was near at hand. By a skilful piece of strategy Washington took possession of Dorchester Heights on the night of the 4th of March, 1776, where earthworks were immediately thrown up, and in the morning the British found their enemy snugly ensconced in a strong position both for offence and defence. A fortunate storm prevented the execution of General Howe's plan of dislodging the Americans; and by the 17th of March his situation in Boston had become so critical that an instant evacuation of the town was imperatively necessary. Before noon of that day the whole British fleet was under sail, and General Washington was marching triumphantly into the town. Our sketch shows the heights of Dorchester as they appear to-day; yet it is easy to see from it how completely the position commands the harbor. No attempt was made

VIEW OF DORCHESTER HEIGHTS.

by the British to repossess the town. At the close of the war Boston was, if not the first town in the country in point of population, the most influential, and it entered immediately upon a course of prosperity that has continued with very few interruptions to the present time.

The first and most serious of these interruptions was that which began with the embargo at the close of the year 1807, and which lasted until the peace of 1815. Massachusetts owned, at the beginning of that disastrous term of seven years, one third of the shipping of the United States. The embargo was a most serious blow to her interests. She did not believe in the constitutionality of the act, nor in its wisdom. She believed that the real motives which were assigned for its passage were not those alleged by the President and the majority in Congress, and this view was confirmed by subsequent events. The war that followed she judged to be a mistake, and her discontent was aggravated by the usurpations of the general government. Nevertheless, in response to the call for troops she sent more men than any other State, and New England furnished more than all the slave States that were so eager in support of the administration. In all the proceedings of those eventful years Boston men were leaders. Holding views that were unpopular, and that many deemed unpatriotic, they held them with pluck and persistence to the end.

Again, in the war of the Rebellion, having been one of the foremost communities in the opposition to slavery, Boston was again a leader, this time on the popular side. In this war, in which she only took part by furnishing men and means to carry it on at a distance, and in supporting it by the cheering and patriotic words of those who remained at home, her history is that of Massachusetts. During the four years of conflict the city and State responded promptly to every call of every nature from the general government, and furnished troops for every department of the army, and money in abundance to carry on the war and to relieve suffering in the field. Boston alone sent into the army and navy no less than 26,119 men, of whom 685 were commissioned officers.

Boston retained its town government until 1822. The subject of changing to the forms of an incorporated city was much discussed as early as 1784, but a vote of the town in favor of the change was not carried until January, 1822, when the citizens declared, by a majority of about six thousand five hundred out of about fifteen thousand votes, their preference for a city government. The Legislature passed an act incorporating the city in February of the same year, and on the 4th of March the charter was formally accepted. The city government, consisting of a mayor, Mr. John Phillips, as chief executive officer, and a city council composed of boards of eight aldermen and forty-eight common councilmen, was organized on May 1.

During the last half-century the commercial importance of Boston has experienced a reasonably steady and constant development. The industries of New England have in that time grown to immense proportions, and Boston is the natural market and distributing point for the most of them. The increase of population and the still more rapid aggregation of wealth tell the story far more effectively than words can do it. In 1790 the population of the town was but eighteen thousand and thirty-three. The combined population of the three towns of Boston, Roxbury, and Dorchester at intervals of ten years, is given in the following table : —

Year.	Population.	Year.	Population.
1800	30,049	1840	107,347
1810	40,386	1850	163,214
1820	51,117	1860	212,746
1830	70,713	1870	250,526

The valuation of real and personal property in the last forty years shows a still more marvellous increase. The official returns at intervals of five years show : —

Year.	Valuation.	Year.	Valuation.
1835	$79,302,600	1855	$241,932,200
1840	94,581,600	1860	278,861,000
1845	135,948,700	1865	371,892,775
1850	180,000,500	1870	584,089,400

In 1840 the average amount of property owned by each inhabitant of Boston was less than nine hundred dollars, but in 1870 it had increased to an average of more than twenty-three hundred dollars. And the value of all the property in Boston is more than seven times as great as it was thirty-five years ago.

The growth of Boston has, notwithstanding these very creditable figures, been very seriously retarded by the lack of room for expansion. Until the era of railroads it was impracticable for gentlemen doing business in Boston to live far from its corporate limits. Accordingly it was necessary to "make land" by filling the flats as soon as the dimensions of the peninsula began to be too contracted for the

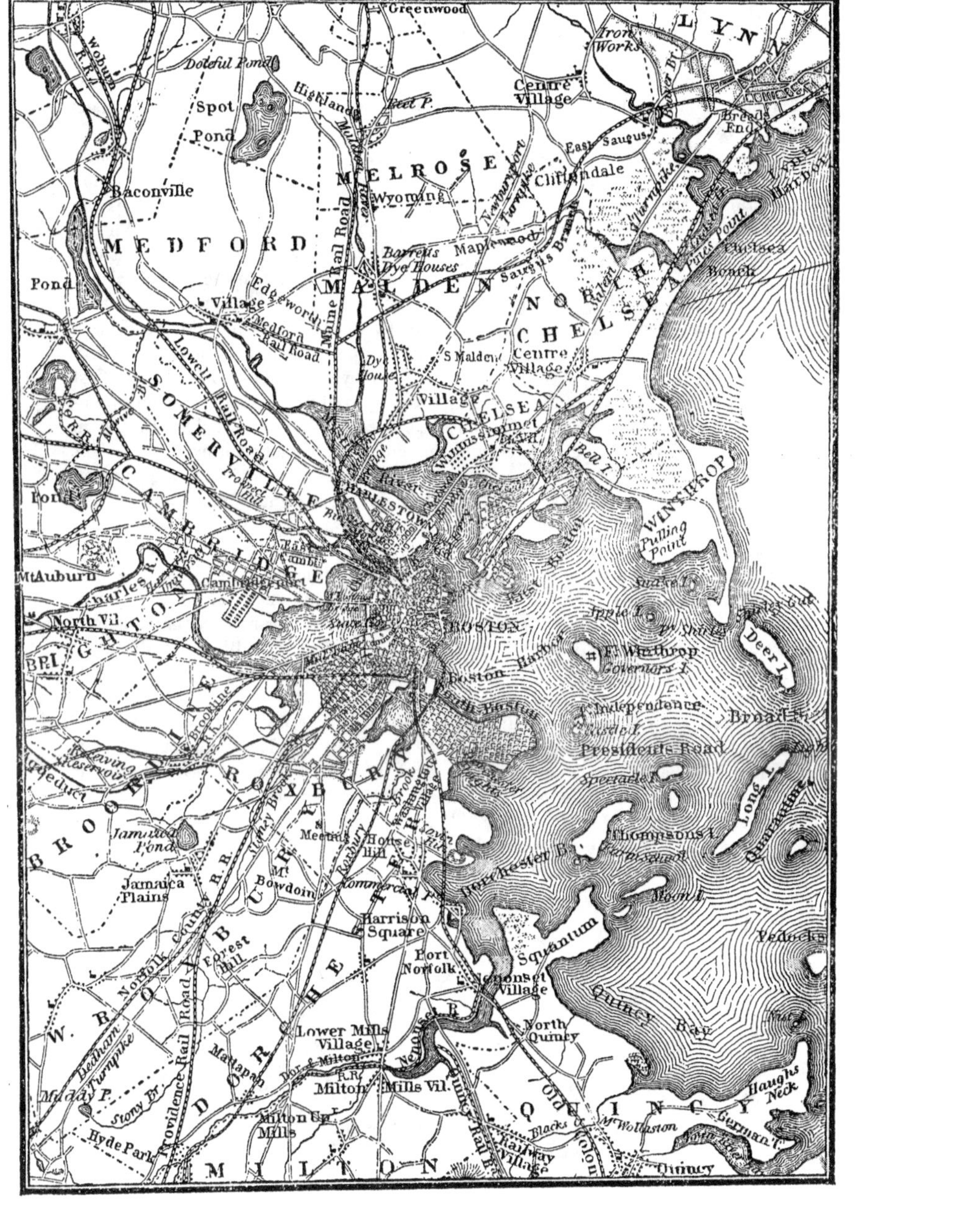

Greenwood
LYNN
Iron Works
Woburn R.R.
Doleful Pond
Spot Pond
Highlands
Beef P.
Centre Village
Breeds End
East Saugus
MELROSE
Cliftondale
Wyoming
Baconville
MEDFORD
Barretts Dye Houses
Maplewood
Saugus Branch
Lynn Harbor
Chelsea Beach
Pond
MALDEN
NORTH CHELSEA
Village
Edgeworth
Medford Rail Road
Lowell Rail Road
S Malden
Centre Village
SOMERVILLE
CHELSEA
Winnissimmet
CAMBRIDGE
Pond
WINTHROP
Pulling Point
Mt Auburn
Cambridgeport
Charles R.
North Vil.
BRIGHTON
BOSTON
Apple I.
Deer I.
Ft. Winthrop
Governors I.
Boston Harbor
South Boston
Ft. Independence
Broad
Presidents Road
Spectacle I.
Long I.
Brookline
Reservoir
ROXBURY
BROOKLINE
Jamaica Pond
Jamaica Plains
Meeting House Hill
Thompsons I.
Dorchester B.
Mt. Bowdoin
Moon I.
Quarantine
Harrison Square
Squantum
Pedocks
Forest Hill
Fort Norfolk
Neponset Village
Norfolk County R.R.
Quincy Bay
North Quincy
Lower Mills Village
Dedham Turnpike
Mattapan
Milton
Mills Vil.
Muddy P.
Stony Br.
Providence Rail Road
DORCHESTER
QUINCY
Haughs Neck
Milton Up. Mills
Hyde Park
Railway Village
Wollaston
MILTON
Quincy

population, and business gathered upon it. Some very old maps show how early this enlargement was commenced; and hardly any two of these ancient charts agree. During the present century very great progress has been made. All the old ponds, coves, and creeks have been filled in, and on the south and southwest the connection with the mainland has been so widened that it is now as broad as the broadest part of the original peninsula; and the work is not yet finished. In other respects the improvements have been immense. All the hills have been cut down, and one of them has been entirely removed. The streets which were formerly so narrow and crooked as to give point to the joke that they were laid out upon the paths made by the cows in going to pasture, have been widened, straightened, and graded. Whole districts covered with buildings of brick and stone have been raised, with the structures upon them, many feet. The city has extended its authority over the island, once known as Noddle's Island, now East Boston, which was almost uninhabited and unimproved until its purchase on speculation in 1830; over South Boston, once Dorchester Neck, annexed to Boston in 1804; and finally, by legislative acts and the consent of the citizens, over the ancient municipalities of Roxbury and Dorchester. The original limits of Boston comprised but six hundred and ninety acres. By filling in flats eight hundred and eighty acres have been added. By the absorption of South and East Boston and by filling the flats surrounding these districts seventeen hundred acres more were acquired, and Roxbury contributed twenty-one hundred acres, and Dorchester forty-eight hundred. The entire present area of the city is therefore ten thousand one hundred and seventy acres, — nearly fifteen times as great as the original area. Meanwhile, the numerous railroads radiating from Boston and reaching to almost every village within thirty miles, have rendered it possible for business men to make their homes far away from their counting-rooms. By this means scores of suburban towns, unequalled in extent and beauty by those surrounding any other great city of the country, have been built up, and the value of property in all the eastern part of Massachusetts has been very largely enhanced. These towns are most intimately connected with Boston in business and social relations, and in a sense form a part of the city. It is this theory that has led to the annexation of Roxbury and Dorchester already, and which will undoubtedly lead at no distant day to the absorption of others of the surrounding cities and towns, in some of which we shall find places and objects to be illustrated and described. The relation of these towns to Boston is shown in the plan on the preceding page.

II. THE NORTH END.

HE extension of the limits of Boston and the movement of business and population to the southward have materially changed the meaning attached to the term North End. In the earliest days of the town, the Mill Creek separated a part of the town from the mainland, and all to the north of it was properly called the North End. For our present purpose we include in that division of the city all the territory north of State, Court, and Cambridge Streets. This district is, perhaps, the richest in historical associations of any part of Boston. It was once the most important part of the town, containing not only the largest warehouses and the public buildings, but the most aristocratic quarter for dwelling-houses. But this was a long time ago. A large part of the North End proper has been abandoned by all residents except the poorest and most vicious classes. Among the important streets may be mentioned Commercial, with its solidly built warehouses, and its great establishments for the sale of grain, ship-chandlery, fish, and other articles; Cornhill, once the head-quarters of the book-trade, and still devoted largely to the same business; the streets radiating from Dock Square, crowded with stores for the sale of cutlery and hardware, meats, wines, groceries, fruit, tin, copper and iron-ware, and other articles of household use; and Hanover, lately widened, and now as formerly a great market for cheap goods of all descriptions. Elsewhere in this district are factories for the production of a variety of articles, from a match to a tombstone, from a set of furniture to a church bell.

There are but a few relics remaining of the North End of the olden time. The streets have been straightened and widened, and go under different names from those first given them, and most of the ancient buildings have fallen to decay and been removed. Among such as are still left to us, the most conspicuous and the most famous is old Faneuil Hall, the "Cradle of Liberty." This building was a gift to the town by Mr. Peter Faneuil. For more than twenty years before its erection the need of a public market had been felt, but the town would never vote to build one. In 1740 Mr. Faneuil offered to build a market at his own expense, and give it to the town, if a vote should be passed to accept it, and keep it open under suitable regulations. This noble offer was accepted by the town, after a hot discussion, by a narrow majority of seven. The building was erected in 1742; and only five years later the opposition to the market-house system was so powerful that a vote was carried to close the market. From that time until 1761 the question whether the market should be open or not was a fruitful source of discord in local politics, each party to the contest scoring several victories. In the last-named year Faneuil Hall was destroyed by fire. This seems to have turned the current of popular opinion in favor of the market, for the town immediately voted to rebuild it. In 1805 it was enlarged to its present size. From the time the Hall was first built until the adoption of the city charter in 1822, all town meetings were held within its walls. In the stirring events that preceded the Revolution it was put to frequent use. The spirited speeches and resolutions ut-

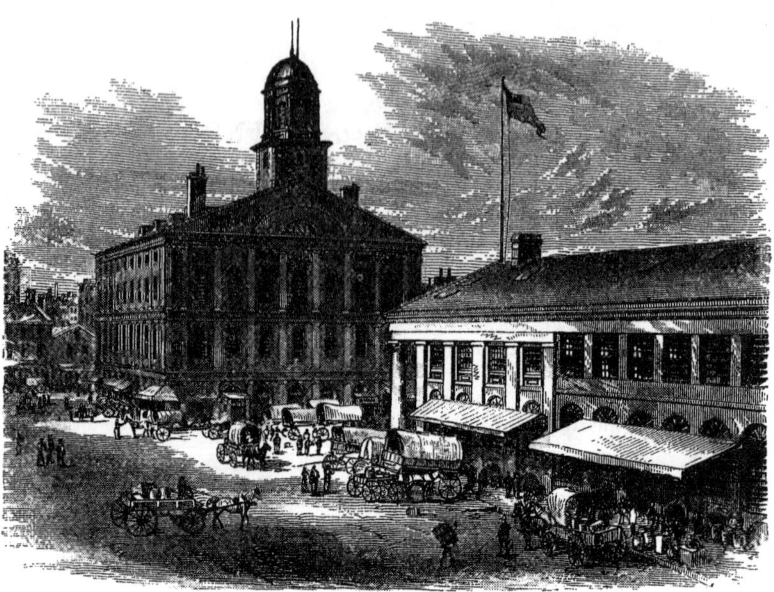

FANEUIL HALL AND QUINCY MARKET.

tered and adopted within it were a most potent agency in exciting the patriotism of all the North American colonists. In every succeeding great crisis in our country's history, thousands of citizens have assembled beneath this roof to listen to the patriotic eloquence of their leaders and counsellors. The great Hall is peculiarly fitted for popular assemblies. It is seventy-six feet square and twenty-eight feet high, and possesses admirable acoustic properties. The floor is left entirely destitute of seats, by which means the capacity of the hall, if not the comfort of audiences, is greatly increased. Numerous large and valuable portraits adorn the walls, — an original full-length painting of Washington, by Stuart; another of the donor of the building, Peter Faneuil, by Colonel Henry Sargent; Healy's great picture of Webster replying to Hayne; excellent portraits of Samuel Adams and the second President Adams; of General Warren and Commodore Preble; of Edward Everett, Abraham Lincoln, and John A. Andrew; and of several others prominent in the history of Massachusetts and the Union. The Hall is never let for money, but it is at the disposal of the people whenever a sufficient number of persons, complying with certain regulations, ask to have it opened. The city charter of Boston, which makes but a very few restrictions upon the right of the city government to govern the city in all local affairs, contains a wise provision forbidding the sale or lease of this Hall.

The new Faneuil Hall Market, popularly known as Quincy Market, originated in a recommendation by Mayor Quincy in 1823. The corner-stone was laid in April, 1825, and the structure was completed in 1827. The building is five hundred and thirty-five feet long and fifty feet wide, and is two stories in height. This great market-house was built at a cost of $150,000, upon made land; and so economically were its affairs managed that the improvement, including the opening of six new streets and the enlargement of a seventh, was accomplished without the levying of any tax, and without any increase of the city's debt.

Quite at the other extreme of our North End district is situated the only other building of a public nature within it to be noticed here, — the Massachusetts General Hospital, — a structure of imposing appearance and devoted to most beneficent uses. This institution had its origin in a bequest of $5,000 made in 1799, but it was not until 1811 that the Hospital was incorporated. The State endowed it with a fee-simple in the old Province House, which was subsequently leased for a term of ninety-nine years. The Massachusetts Hospital Life Insurance Company was required by its charter to pay one third of its net profits to the Hospital. Large sums of money were raised by private subscription both before the institution had begun operations and every year since. On the 1st of January, 1872, the general fund of the Hospital amounted to $888,258.17; the total of restricted funds at the same date being $470,533.78. The aggregate of funds not invested in real estate was $559,046.85. During the preceding year the income of the corporation was $211,302.41, and the expenses amounted to $238,458.45. These figures are for the Hospital proper, and for the McLean Asylum for the Insane at Somerville, which is a branch of the institution.

THE MASSACHUSETTS GENERAL HOSPITAL.

The handsome granite building west of Blossom Street was erected in 1818, and enlarged by the addition of two extensive wings in 1846. The stone of the original building was hammered and fitted by the convicts at the State Prison. The system on which this noble institution is managed is admirable, in that it is so designed as to combine the principles of gratuitous treatment and the payment of their expenses by those who are able to do so. The hospital turns none away who come within the scope of its operations, while it has room to receive them, however poor they may be. It has been greatly aided in its work by the generous contributions and bequests of wealthy people. The fund permanently invested to furnish free beds amounts to more than $375,000, and the annual contributions for free beds during the year 1871 supported one hundred and seventeen of them at $100 each. To those who are able to pay for their board and for medical treatment the charges are in all cases moderate, never exceeding the actual expense. During the last year more than fifteen hundred patients were treated for a longer or a shorter time, of whom more than two thirds were treated free. This number, however, represents only such as were admitted into the hospital; nearly ten thousand out-patients also received advice, medicine, or surgical or dental treatment. It will show more clearly how great good is done precisely where it is most needed, if we say that out of 889 male patients admitted to the wards during the year, 660 were classed as mechanics, laborers, seamen, teamsters, and servants; while of 539 female patients, 317 were classed as domestics, seamstresses, and operatives. Statistics sometimes tell a story of good work well done more graphically than pages of eloquent praise, and this is true of this noble institution.

Four of the eight railroads terminating in Boston have their stations in this part of the city, — three of them within a stone's throw of each other, on Causeway Street. Our view represents the stations of the Eastern and Fitchburg Railroads, with a section of the new Lowell station in the foreground. The former is an unpretentious building of brick, erected in 1863, after the destruction by fire of the former station, and is small and inadequate to do the immense business which the Eastern road has built up. Measures are now in progress to substitute a new and larger station. The Eastern Railroad, by arrangement with the Maine Central Railroad, now runs its cars through to Bangor, Me., there making close connection with the railroad to St. John, New Brunswick. In addition to the extensive through travel thus secured, it performs an exceedingly large amount of local business for the cities and towns along the coast to Portsmouth. In 1847 the total number of passengers carried on this line was but 651,408. The number carried during the year ending September 30, 1871, was 4,610,277.

EASTERN AND FITCHBURG RAILROAD STATIONS.

The station of the Fitchburg Railroad is represented at the extreme right hand of our sketch. It was built in 1847, the terminus of the road having previously been in Charlestown. In a great hall in the upper part of this structure, two grand concerts were given by Jenny Lind in October, 1850, to audiences numbering on each occasion more than four thousand people. The agents of Mr. Barnum, who was at that time paying her $1,000 for each concert, sold, for the second concert, tickets to a thousand more people than could be accommodated. The manager was accordingly obliged to refund the money the next day, to his own chagrin and to the infinite disgust of those who had failed to hear the great Swedish singer. Even with the disappointed thousand excluded, the hall was so densely packed that very many ladies fainted, and there was at times serious danger of a panic. The newspapers of the day remarked with admiration upon the magical effect of Jenny Lind's voice in calming and restoring to order the crowded multitude. The Fitchburg Railroad passes through several important suburban towns, and transacts an extensive local and through business. Upon the completion of the Hoosac Tunnel, by which time the entire line to Troy, N. Y., will probably be consolidated, it is expected that the Fitchburg road will become a very important route for passengers and freight from the West.

Our sketch of the Lowell Railroad Station is of the station that is to be, and that is now rapidly constructing. When completed it will be inferior in size to very few railroad stations in the country, and second to none in elegance and the provisions made for the comfort of travellers. It is to be seven hundred feet long, and will have a front of two hundred and five feet on Causeway Street; the material is to be face brick with trimmings of Nova Scotia freestone. The engraving shows the elegance of the building; but it cannot display the great arch of the train-house, which has a clear span of one hundred and twenty feet without any central support. This train-house will shortly be ready for use, but the entire structure will not be finished until the fall of 1873. The Lowell Railroad, by its connection with routes to Montreal and the West, has secured a very large through business, in addition to its great and increasing local traffic.

BOSTON AND LOWELL RAILROAD STATION.

The Boston and Maine Railroad, alone of all the lines entering the city on the north side, enjoys the privilege of penetrating within the outer street. Its station is in Haymarket Square, and the open space in front of it gives prominence to the structure. The station has within two or three years been greatly enlarged and improved, so that it is now, internally, one of the lightest and pleasantest edifices of the

HAYMARKET SQUARE.

kind in the city. The Maine road has a very large local business, serving the towns of Malden, Melrose, Reading, Wakefield, and Andover, and the cities of Haverhill and Lawrence. At present it extends only to South Berwick, in Maine, where it joins the Eastern Railroad; but the line to Portland is rapidly building, and will soon be opened.

The old North Burying-ground, on Copp's Hill, was the second established in the town. Its original limits, when first used for interments in 1660, were much smaller

COPP'S HILL BURYING-GROUND.

than now, and the enclosure did not reach its present size until about forty years ago. Like most of the remaining relics of the early times, this burial-ground bears traces of the Revolutionary contest. The British soldiers occupied it as a military station, and used to amuse themselves by firing bullets at the gravestones. The marks made in this sacrilegious sport may still be discovered by careful examination of the stones. One of these most defaced is that above the grave of Captain Daniel Malcom, which bears an inscription speaking of him as "A TRUE SON OF LIBERTY A FRIEND TO THE PUBLICK AN ENEMY TO OPPRESSION AND ONE OF THE FOREMOST IN OPPOSING THE REVENUE ACTS ON AMERICA."

This refers to a bold act of Captain Malcom, in landing a valuable cargo of wines, in 1768, without paying the duty upon it. This was done in the night under the guard of bands of men armed with clubs. It would be called smuggling at the present day, but when committed it was deemed a laudable and patriotic act, because the tax was regarded as unjust, oppressive, and illegal. The most noted persons whose bodies repose within this enclosure were undoubtedly the three Reverend Doctors Mather, — Increase, Cotton, and Samuel; but there are many curious and interesting inscriptions to read, which would well repay a visit. The burying-ground is even now a favorite place of resort in the warmer months, and the gates stand hospitably open to callers, though they have long been closed against the admission of new inhabitants. It is to the credit of the city, that, when it became necessary in the improvement of that section of the city to cut down the hill to some extent, the burying-ground was left untouched, and the embankment protected by a high stone-wall.

Two of the leading hotels of Boston are in this district of the city. The American House, on Hanover St., is the largest public house in New England, and one of the best. Its external appearance has been very greatly improved by the recent widening of Hanover Street. It covers the sites of four former hotels,—Earle's, the Merchants', the Hanover, and the old American Houses. It was rebuilt in 1851, and numerous additions have been made since. The interior has also been completely remodelled within a few years, and many of the rooms are exceedingly elegant, while the furniture of the house is throughout handsome and substantial. A splendid passenger elevator was added to the house when it was refitted, and as the furnishing of the rooms is uniform on all the floors, the highest rooms are as desirable as those on the second story. The grand dining-room is an immense hall, capable of seating at one time more than three hundred people; when lighted at night it is one of the most brilliant halls in Boston, having at either end mammoth mirrors reaching from the floor to the ceiling. The American has long been a favorite resort for strangers in the city on business, and it is practically the headquarters of the shoe and leather trade. It has been under one management for thirty-five years.

The Revere House is not strictly within the limits of the district we have drawn, but it is separated from that district only by the width of a single street. It is a building of fine appearance, as will be seen from our sketch. It was erected by the Massachusetts Charitable Mechanic Association, and was for a long time under the management of the veteran Paran Stevens. It was, of course, named in memory of Paul Revere, the patriotic mechanic of Boston before and during the Revolution, and the first president of the Charitable Mechanic Association. Colonel Revere was a companion and fellow-worker with Samuel Adams, James Otis, Joseph Warren, and others of the leaders of opinion in the days of Stamp and Tea Acts. He helped the cause in various ways, — by engraving with friendly but unskilful hand the portraits of Adams and others; by casting church bells to be rung and cannon to be fired; by printing paper money, which was, however, neither a valuable currency nor a commendable work of art; by words and deeds of patriotism that entitle him to grateful remembrance by all Americans. The versatile colonel appears in the first Directory of Boston, for 1789, as a goldsmith doing business at No. 50 Cornhill, — now Washington Street. The hotel

which bears his name has entertained more distinguished men than any other in Boston. The Prince of Wales occupied apartments in the Revere on his visit to the city twelve years ago. President Grant has been a guest of the house, and in the winter of 1871 it was the head-quarters of the Grand Duke Alexis of Russia. The Revere is situated in Bowdoin Square.

During the past year one of the old landmarks of the north part of the city has been in process of demolition. The church in Brattle Square was long known as the Manifesto Church, the original members having put forth in 1699, just before their church was dedicated, a document declaring their aims and purposes. While themselves adopting the belief which was then universal among the Congregational churches of the time, they conceded the right of difference of belief among the members. What Congregational churches were to those ruled by ecclesiastical superiors, or by convocations, the individual member of the Manifesto Church was to be to the members of other Congregational churches, and the distinction between church and congregation was abolished. Expecting a difficulty in getting ordained in Boston, their first minister was ordained in London. The modest church edifice built in 1699 was taken down in 1772, and the building just demolished, erected on the same spot, was dedicated on the 25th of July, 1773. During the Revolution the pastor, who was a patriot, was obliged to leave Boston, services were suspended, and the British soldiery used the building as a barrack. A cannon-ball from a battery in Cambridge struck the church, on the night before the evacuation of Boston; and this memento of the glorious contest was afterwards built into the external wall of the church, above the porch. Among the long line of eminent clergymen who have been pastors of this church, may be mentioned the late Edward Everett, who is so much better known as a statesman than as a minister that the fact of his having been a clergyman is frequently forgotten. The old church was sold in 1871, and the

BRATTLE SQUARE CHURCH.

last service was held in it July 30 of that year, a memorial sermon being preached on that occasion by the pastor, the Rev. Dr. S. K. Lothrop. The ancient pulpit, the old bell, the organ, the historic cannon-ball, and some other mementoes, were reserved at the sale. The society is now erecting a large and elegant structure at the corner of Commonwealth Avenue and Clarendon Street.

The oldest church in the city is Christ Church, Episcopal, on Salem Street. The Episcopalian denomination was for a long time of slow growth in Boston; but in 1723, notwithstanding the enlargement of King's Chapel, then a society of the Church of England, in 1710 the number of Church people was so large that it was necessary to found a new society. The corner-stone was laid in April, 1723, and the church was dedicated in December of the same year. This is the first and only building ever occupied by the society. During the Revolution, the rector of Christ Church, the Rev. Mather Byles, Jr., left the town on account of his sympathy with the royal cause. The steeple of this church is a very prominent landmark, and is one of the most noticeable features in approaching the city from the harbor. It is, however, but a copy, as accurate as could be made, of the original steeple, which was blown down in the great gale of October, 1804. The tower contains a fine chime of eight bells, upon which have been rung joyful and mournful peals for more than a century and a quarter.

CHRIST CHURCH, SALEM STREET.

Only one of the great daily newspapers of the city is published within the North End district, — the Daily Advertiser. The Advertiser is the oldest daily paper in Boston, having nearly reached the sixtieth year of continuous publication. It is a little curious that the site now occupied by the Advertiser as a permanent home, after a protracted period of migration, is that from which James Franklin issued the first number of the New England Courant, in 1721. The same spot was again occupied by a printing-office in 1776, by the Independent Chronicle, which was suspended during the Revolution. The Advertiser has succeeded to the rights of the Chronicle, and therefore considers that when it took possession of its present building, in 1867,

—a building, by the way, admirably suited to its purpose,—it merely returned to its first home. The first number of the Daily Advertiser ever published thus announced the character of the paper: "The predominant feature of the Daily Advertiser will be commercial,—yet it will be by no means destitute of a political character." This promise it has kept strictly. At times it has fallen behind some of its contemporaries in enterprise, but within the last eight or ten years it has resumed once more its old place among the foremost journals of New England.

At the head of Washington Street, in a most conspicuous position, stands the great printing establishment of Rand, Avery, & Co. The office was established many years ago, and was very small at first, but has gradually grown to its present immense proportions. The building in which this firm is located stands six stories high on Cornhill and Washington Street, seven stories high on Brattle Street, and is over one hundred and fifty feet long. In this building every part of the art of book-making is performed,—type-setting, stereotyping, presswork, and binding. More than two hundred persons are constantly employed, and nearly as many more are in one way or another dependent upon the vast business transacted here,—the establishment being one of the largest printing-offices in the country. The processes of book-making are very interesting under any circumstances, and they are doubly so when they are transacted on a large scale, with all the appliances of modern machinery.

At this point Washington Street makes a curious short curve to the right, and terminates in Dock Square. It has long been suggested to continue Washington Street through to the northern part of the city, giving a more direct as well as a wider avenue to the railroad stations and to Charlestown than at present exists. This plan has been urged more persistently of late than ever before. In case it should be carried out, the extension of the street would pass directly through the fine building represented in the accompanying view.

VIEW AT THE HEAD OF WASHINGTON STREET.

III. THE WEST END.

T was, perhaps, fortunate for the people of Boston that the original peninsula was so uneven of surface. The physical geography of the town determined the laws of its growth and development. It was inevitable that the business of Boston in its early days, being chiefly commercial, should cluster near the wharves. It was natural that the high hills should be chosen for residences. When, in the progress of the town, the merchants burst through the ancient limits of trade, they insensibly followed the line of level ground, and left the hills covered with dwelling-houses. It was not until Fort Hill had been wholly surrounded by mercantile houses that the people residing upon that once beautiful eminence reluctantly retired. It is only within a few years that the quieter branches of business — agencies, architects' and lawyers' offices — have begun to mount Beacon Hill, and the progress is so slow that there seems but little prospect that a business movement in that direction will meet with much success. From the difficulty that business almost always experiences in ascending a hill has resulted the preservation of a very large section of the city in the immediate neighborhood of business, which is still, and is likely to remain, a desirable place for residences. This section is generally called the West End, — a term which is, like the North End, very difficult to be defined. We have already included in the latter division a part of what is usually termed the West End, and we must now, for convenience' sake, embrace within the limits of the West End a part of the South End. Our division includes all that part of the city south and west of Cambridge, Court, and Tremont Streets, to the line of the Boston and Albany Railroad, following the line of that railroad to Brookline. These boundaries take in the whole of Beacon Hill, the Common and Public Garden, and most of the Back Bay new land.

It has already been said that Beacon Hill, the highest in Boston, has been shorn of its original proportions. It is to-day neither very steep nor very high, nor is it easy to convey any intelligible idea of its original character by giving the altitude of its highest point above the level of the sea. Those who are familiar with the neighborhood will understand the extent of the changes, however, when it is said that the three peaks of "Trea Mount" were where Pemberton Square, the Reservoir, and Louisburg Square now are. The hill was cut down in the early years of the present century, and Mount Vernon Street was laid out at that time; but it was not until 1835 that the hill where Pemberton Square now is was removed, and that square laid out. Beacon Hill obtained its name from the fact that, for almost a century and a half from the settlement of the town, a tall pole stood upon its summit, surmounted by a skillet filled with tar, to be fired in case it was desired to give an alarm to the surrounding towns. After the Revolution a monument took its place, which stood until 1811, and was then taken down to make room for improvements.

The highest point of the hill in its present shape is occupied by the Massachusetts State House, an illustration of which is given on the cover of this book. So prominent is its position that it is impossible to make a comprehensive sketch of the city that does not exhibit the dome of the State House as the central point of the background. The land on which it stands was formerly Governor Hancock's cow-pasture, and was bought of his heirs by the town and given to the State. The corner-stone was laid by the Freemasons, Paul Revere grand master, in 1793, Governor Samuel Adams being present and making an address on the occasion. It was first occupied by the Legislature in January, 1798. In 1852 it was enlarged at the rear by an extension northerly to Mount Vernon Street, an improvement which cost considerably more than the entire first cost of the building. In 1866 and 1867 it was very extensively remodelled inside.

There are a great many points of interest about the State House. The statues of Webster and Mann, on either side of the approach to the building, will attract notice, if not always admiration. Within the Doric Hall, or rotunda, hours may be spent by the stranger in examining the objects that deserve attention. Here is the fine statue of Washington, by Chantrey; here are arranged in an attractive manner, behind glass protectors, the battle-flags borne by Massachusetts soldiers in the war against Rebellion; here are copies of the tombstones of the Washington family in Brington Parish, England, presented to Senator Sumner by an English nobleman, and by the former to the State; here is the admirable statue of Governor Andrew; here are the busts of the patriot hero Samuel Adams, of the martyred President Lincoln, and of Senator Sumner; near by are the tablets taken from the monument just mentioned which was erected on Beacon Hill after the Revolution to commemorate that contest. Ascending into the Hall of Representatives, we find suspended from the ceiling the ancient codfish, emblem of the direction taken by Massachusetts industry in the early times. In the Senate Chamber there are also relics of the olden time and portraits of distinguished men. From the cupola, which is always open when the General Court is not in session, is to be obtained one of the finest views of Boston and the neighboring country. A register of the visitors to the cupola is kept in a book prepared for the purpose. During the last season, between the 6th of June and the 22d of December, no less than 42,990 persons ascended the long flights of stairs to obtain this view of Boston and its suburbs, an average of three hundred a day.

The statue of Governor Andrew in Doric Hall is one of the most excellent of our portrait statues. It represents the great war governor as he appeared before care had ploughed its lines in his face. This statue was first unveiled to public view when it was presented to the State on the 14th of February, 1871. Its history is as follows: In January, 1865, a meeting was held in Faneuil Hall, at which it was voted to raise a fund for the erection of a statue to the late Edward Everett. The response was much more liberal than was necessary for the original purpose, and after the statue on the Public Garden, to be mentioned hereafter, was finished, a large surplus remained. The portrait of Everett now in Faneuil Hall was procured and paid for, a considerable sum was voted in aid of the equestrian statue of Washington, and of the balance, ten thousand dollars were appropriated for a statue of Andrew, which the State subsequently passed a formal vote to accept. The artist was Thomas Ball, a native of Charlestown, but now resident in Florence. The marble is of beautiful texture and whiteness, and the statue is approved both for its admirable likeness of the eminent original and for its artistic merits.

THE ANDREW STATUE.

There is nothing in Boston of which Bostonians are more truly proud than of the Common. Other cities have larger and more pretentious public grounds ; none of them can boast a park of greater natural beauty, or better suited to the purposes to which it is put. There are no magnificent drives, for teams are not admitted within the sacred precincts. Everything is of the plainest and homeliest character. A part of the Common is left to itself, and is as barren as the feet of ten thousand youthful ball-players can make it. There is the Frog Pond, with its fountain, where the boys may sail their miniature ships at their own sweet will. There is the deer park, a delightful and popular resort for the youngest of the visitors to this noble public space. All the malls and paths are shaded by fine old trees, which have their names somewhat pedantically labelled upon them, giving an admirable opportunity for the study of what we may call grand botany. On bright spring days the Common is resorted to by thousands of boys, who find here ample room to give vent to their surplus spirit and animation, free from all undue restraint. On summer evenings the throng of promenaders is very great, and of itself testifies to the value placed by all classes upon this opportunity to get a breath of fresh air in the heart of the city.

The history of the Common has been written several times, but there are nevertheless curiously erroneous notions prevalent in regard to the manner in which it became public ground, and the power of the city over it. The territory of Boston was purchased from Mr. Blaxton by the corporation of colonists who settled it. The land was then divided among the several inhabitants by the officers of the town. A part of it was set off as a training-field and as common ground, subject originally to further division in case such a course should be thought advisable. In 1640 a vote was passed by the town, in consequence of a movement on the part of certain citizens that was discovered and thwarted none too soon, that, with the exception of "3 or 4 lotts to make vp ye streete from bro Robte Walkers to ye Round Marsh," no more land should be granted out of the Common. It is solely by the power of this vote and the jealousy of the citizens sustaining it that the Common was kept sacred to the uses of the people as a whole from 1640 until the adoption of the city charter, when, by the desire of the citizens, and by the consent of the Legislature, the right to alienate any portion of the Common was expressly withheld from the city government.

THE FROG POND.

The earliest use to which the Common was put was that of a pasture and a training-field on muster days. The occupation of the Common as a grazing-field continued until the year 1830, but it was by no means wholly given up to that use. As early as 1675 an English traveller, Mr. John Josselyn, published in London an "Account of Two Voyages," in which occurs the following notice of Boston Common: "On the south there is a small but pleasant Common, where the Gallants a little before sunset walk with their *Marmalet*-Madams, as we do in Moorfields, etc., till the nine a clock Bell rings them home to their respective habitations, when presently the Constables walk their rounds to see good orders kept, and to take up loose people." Previous and long subsequent to this the Common was also the usual place for executions. Four persons at least were hanged for witchcraft between 1656 and 1660. Murderers, pirates, deserters, and others were put to death under the forms of law upon the Common, until, in 1812, a memorial signed by a great number of citizens induced the selectmen to order that no part of the Common should be granted for such a purpose. Those who have studied the history of Boston most closely are of opinion that on more than one occasion a branch of the great Elm was used as the gallows. And near that famous tree was the scene of a lamentable duel, in 1728, that resulted in the death of a very promising young man. The level ground east of Charles Street has been used from the very earliest times as a parade-ground. Here take place the annual parade and drum-head election of the Ancient and Honorable Artillery Company, the oldest military organization in the country, and here the Governor delivers to the newly elected officers their commissions for the year.

The original boundary of the Common was quite different from the present. On the west it was bounded by the low lands and flats of the Back Bay ; on the north by Beacon Street to Tremont Street ; thence by an irregular line to West Street ; and thence to the corner of Boylston and Carver Streets, and upon that line to the water. Upon that part bounded by Park, Beacon, and Tremont Streets were once situated the granary, the almshouse, the workhouse, and the bridewell. In 1733 a way was established across the Common where Park Street (which was formerly called Centry Street) now is. Since the establishment of that street, the land occupied by the institutions above named has been sold for private purposes. Compensation has been made to some extent by the addition of the land in the angle between Tremont and Boylston Streets. The land for the burying-ground was bought by the town in 1757, and that part where is now situated the deer park in 1787. On the west a considerable piece was cut off when Charles Street was laid out, in 1803, but here also there was rather a gain than a loss, since the piece so amputated was enlarged by filling flats, and added to the public grounds. The area of the Common is now very nearly forty-eight acres.

It would be impossible within our limits to mention all that is of interest upon and about the Common ; but some things cannot be passed over. The Old Elm is perhaps the chief object of interest still, though its symmetrical beauty is gone. This great tree is certainly the oldest known tree in New England. It was large enough to find a place on the map engraved in 1722, and on the great branch broken off by the gale of 1860 could be easily counted nearly two hundred rings, carrying the age of that branch back to 1670. It is surmised that the supposed witch, Ann Hibbens, was hanged upon it in 1656, and if so, it could have hardly been less than twenty-six years old, which would make the Old Elm as old as the town of Boston. Great care has been taken to preserve this tree. A gale in 1832 caused it much injury, and the limbs were restored to their former places at great cost and with much labor, after which they were secured by iron bands and bars. The great

THE OLD ELM, BOSTON COMMON.

gale of June, 1860, tore off the largest limb and otherwise mutilated it, and again it was restored as far as was possible, and the cavity was filled up and covered. In September, 1869, the high wind that tore the roof from the first Coliseum and blew down the spires of so many churches in Boston and vicinity, made havoc with the remaining limbs, taking off one great branch that was forty-two inches in circumference. The iron fence around the tree was put up in 1854.

The Frog Pond was, probably, in the early days of Boston, just what its name indicates, — a low, marshy spot, filled with stagnant water, and the abode of the tuneful batrachian. The enterprise of the early inhabitants is credited with having transformed it into a real artificial pond. This pond was the scene of the formal introduction of the water of Cochituate Lake into Boston, on the 25th of October, 1848. A great procession was organized on that day, under the direction of the city government, which marched through the principal streets to the Common, where, after a hymn sung by the Handel and Haydn Society, a prayer, an ode written by James Russell Lowell and sung by the school-children, addresses by the Hon. Nathan Hale and by Mayor Quincy, the water was let on through the gate of the fountain, amid the shouts of the people, the roar of cannon, the hiss of rockets, and the ringing of bells.

The burying-ground on Boylston Street, formerly known as the South, and later as the Central Burying-ground, is the least interesting of the old cemeteries of Boston. It was opened in 1756, but the oldest stone, with the exception of one which was removed from some other ground, or which perpetuates a manifest error, is dated 1761. The best-known name upon any stone in the graveyard is that of Monsieur Julien, the inventor of the famous soup that bears his name, and the most noted restaurateur of Boston in the last century.

One of the most conspicuous objects on the Common is the Brewer fountain, the gift to the city of Gardner Brewer, Esq., which began to play for the first time on June 3, 1868. It is a copy, in bronze, of a fountain designed by the French artist Liénard, executed for the Paris World's Fair of 1855, where it was awarded a gold medal. The great figures at the base represent Neptune and Amphitrite, Acis and Galatea. The fountain was cast in Paris, and was procured, brought to this country, and set up at the sole expense of the public-spirited donor. Copies in iron have been made for the cities of Lyons and Bordeaux; and an exact copy, in bronze, of the fountain on the Common was made for Said Pacha, the late Viceroy of Egypt.

THE BREWER FOUNTAIN.

Upon the old Flagstaff Hill, close by the Frog Pond and the Old Elm, will stand the Soldiers' Monument, the corner-stone of which was laid with appropriate ceremonies September 18, 1871. Upon a granite platform will rest the plinth, in the form of a Greek cross, with four panels in which will be inserted bas-reliefs representing the Sanitary Commission, the Navy, the Departure for the War, and the Return. At each of the four corners will be a statue of heroic size, representing Peace, History, the Army, and the Navy. The die upon the plinth will also be richly sculptured, and upon it, surrounding the shaft in alto-relievo, will be four allegorical figures, representing the North, South, East, and West. The shaft is to be a Roman Doric column, the whole to be surmounted by a colossal statue of America, resting on a hemisphere, guarded by four figures of the American eagle, with outspread wings. "America" will hold in her left hand the national standard, and in her right she will support a sheathed sword and wreaths for the victors. The extreme height of the monument will be ninety feet, and it will not be completed for a year or more. The artist is Mr. Martin Millmore, of Boston.

There are very few spots on the Common with which some Bostonian has not a pleasant association. Almost every citizen and visitor has rejoiced in the grateful shade of the Tremont Street Mall, or the arching elms of the Beacon Street Mall, on a hot summer's day. Few would care to tramp upon the burning bricks of the sidewalks when there is so pleasant a path close at hand. But the associations are by no means confined to the mere experience of comfort beneath the shadow of these wide-spreading trees. How many thousand "gallants" have walked these malls with their "marmalet-madams," holding sweet converse the while! The inimitable Dr. Holmes has laid the scene of one of the pleasantest courtships in literature at the head of one of the malls branching from the one which our view represents. The "autocrat of the breakfast-table" had engaged passage for Liverpool, that he might escape forever from the sight of the fascinating

BEACON STREET MALL.

schoolmistress if she turned a deaf ear to his petition. Having thus provided a way of escape, he planned to take a walk with her.

"It was on the Common that we were walking. The *mall*, or boulevard of our Common, you know, has various branches leading from it in different directions. One of these runs down from opposite Joy Street, southward across the length of the whole Common to Boylston Street. We called it the long path, and were fond of it.

"I felt very weak, indeed, (though of a tolerably robust habit,) as we came opposite the head of this path on that morning. I think I tried to speak twice without making myself distinctly audible. At last I got out the question, 'Will you take the long path with me?' 'Certainly,' said the schoolmistress, 'with much pleasure.' 'Think,' I said, 'before you answer; if you take the long path with me now, I shall interpret it that we are to part no more!' The schoolmistress stepped back with a sudden movement, as if an arrow had struck her.

"One of the long granite blocks used as seats was hard by, the one you may still see close by the Ginko tree. 'Pray, sit down,' I said. 'No, no,' she answered, softly, 'I will walk the *long path* with you.'"

The history of the Public Garden is shorter and less interesting than that of the Common. Before the improvement of this part of the city was begun, a large part

THE PUBLIC GARDEN, FROM ARLINGTON STREET.

of what is now the Public Garden was covered by the tides, and the rest was known as "the marsh at the foot of the Common." In 1794, the ropewalks having been burned, the town voted to grant these flats for the erection of new ropewalks. It was not until many years later that the folly of this act was seen, — indeed, not until after the construction of the Mill-dam, now the extension of Beacon Street, to

Brookline. When the tide had ceased to flow freely over the flats, and the marsh so rashly granted became dry land, the holders of this property, having once more lost their rope-walks by fire, in 1819, began to realize its value, and proposed to sell it for business and dwelling purposes. Charles Street had been laid out in 1803, and this increased the value of building-lots on the tract, if it could be sold. The proposed action was, however, resisted, and finally, in 1824, the city paid upwards of fifty thousand dollars to regain what the town had in a fit of generosity given away. But for a long

THE POND, PUBLIC GARDEN.

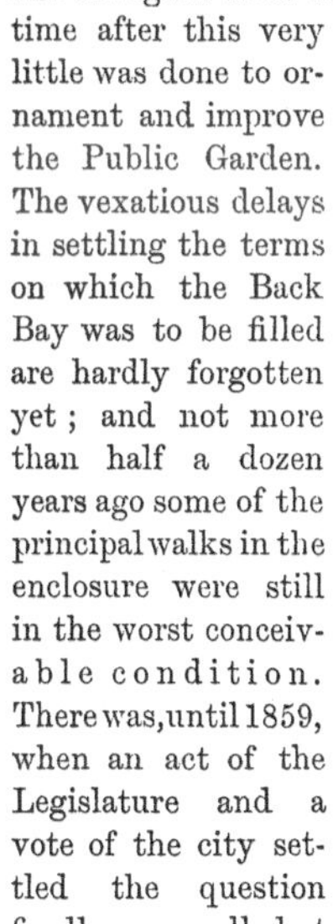

time after this very little was done to ornament and improve the Public Garden. The vexatious delays in settling the terms on which the Back Bay was to be filled are hardly forgotten yet; and not more than half a dozen years ago some of the principal walks in the enclosure were still in the worst conceivable condition. There was, until 1859, when an act of the Legislature and a vote of the city settled the question finally, a small but

THE BRIDGE, PUBLIC GARDEN.

earnest party in favor of disposing of the entire tract for building purposes, —just as there is now a persistent class of persons who desire the improvement of several streets at the expense of the Common. All these unwise plans failed, and the Public Garden became the inalienable property of the city. In the last thirteen years very much has been done to make the Public Garden attractive, and although it has not the diversified surface and shaded walks of the older enclosure, it has already become a favorite resort for young and old.

The area of this park is about twenty-one and a quarter acres. It is not exactly rectangular in shape, as it seems to be, the Boylston Street side being longer than the Beacon Street, and the Charles Street longer than the Arlington Street side. The pond in the centre is laboriously irregular in shape, and is wholly artificial. It contains rather less than four acres, and was constructed in 1859, almost immediately after the act of the Legislature relating to the Public Garden had been accepted. The central walk, from Charles to Arlington Streets, crosses this pond by an iron bridge resting on granite piers, erected in 1867. The appearance of unnecessary solidity and strength which this bridge presents gave point to numerous jokes in the newspapers of the day. The bridge is certainly strong enough to support an army on the march, and perhaps it looks much more substantial than it really is ; but aside from the rather ponderous appearance of the piers, there is very little opportunity for unfavorable criticism of the structure.

There are several interesting works of art in the Public Garden. The one first placed there was a small but very beautiful statue of Venus rising from the Sea, which stands near the Arlington Street entrance, opposite Commonwealth Avenue. The fountain connected with this statue is so arranged as to throw, when it is playing, a fine spray all about the figure of Venus, producing a remarkably beautiful effect. Further on towards Beacon Street stands the monument to the discovery and to the discoverer, whoever he may be, of anæsthetics, presented by Thomas Lee, Esq., and dedicated in June, 1868. In the centre of the Beacon Street side stands the statue in bronze of the late Edward Everett. The funds for this statue were raised by a public subscription, in 1865. The remarkable success of this subscription has already been referred to. This statue was modelled in Rome by Story, in 1866, cast in Munich, and presented to the city in November, 1867. The orator stands with his head thrown back, and with his right arm extended in the act of making a favorite and graceful gesture.

THE EVERETT STATUE.

But the most conspicuous of all the works of art in the Public Garden is Ball's great equestrian statue of Washington, which is justly regarded by many as one of the finest, as it is one of the largest, pieces of the kind in America. The movement which resulted in the erection of this monument was begun in the spring of 1859.

The earliest contribution to the fund was the proceeds of an oration delivered by the Hon. Robert C. Winthrop in the Music Hall less than a month after the committee was organized. A great fair held in the same place in November of the same year, and an appropriation of ten thousand dollars from the city, supplied the greater part of the needful funds, supplemented in 1868 by a contribution of five thousand dollars of the surplus remaining after the erection of the statue of Everett just mentioned. The contract for the statue was made with Thomas Ball in December, 1859, and the model was completed in a little more than four years. The war was then waging, and the foundries were all engaged upon work for the government. It was not until 1867 that a contract was made for the casting with the Ames Manufacturing Company, of Chicopee. The statue was unveiled on the 3d of July, 1869. It is a matter of no little local pride that all the artists and artisans employed in its production were furnished by Massachusetts, without any help from abroad. The statue represents Washington at a different period of his life from that usually selected by artists, and is all the more effective and original on that account. The outline is graceful, and perfectly natural from every point of view, and the work reveals new beauties the more it is examined. It was cast in fourteen pieces, but the joints are invisible. The extreme height of the pedestal and statue is thirty-eight feet, the statue itself being twenty-two feet high. The foundation, which rests upon piles, is of solid masonry, eleven feet deep. The lamented Governor Andrew was one of the original committee which undertook the direction of this work, but he died before its completion.

THE WASHINGTON STATUE.

Close by one of the busiest spots in Boston is one of those ancient landmarks which the good sense and the good taste of its citizens have thus far preserved. It has been remarked that the irregular piece of territory bounded by Beacon, Tremont, and Park Streets was originally a part of the Common. In 1660 it became necessary to appropriate new space to resting-places for the dead, and the thrifty habits of our forefathers would not suffer them to buy land for the purpose when they were already in possession of a great tract lying in common. Accordingly, in the year before mentioned, the graveyard now known as the Old Granary Burying-ground was established. Two years afterwards, other portions of the territory now lost to the Common were appropriated for sites for the bridewell, house of correction, almshouse, and public granary. The last-named building, which stood at first near the head of Park Street, and afterwards on the present site of the meeting-house, gave to the burying-ground the name by which it is so commonly designated. This is, without exception, the most interesting of the old Boston graveyards. Within this little enclosure lie the remains of some of the most eminent men in the history of Massachusetts and the country. The list includes no less than nine Governors of the Colony and State; two of the signers of the Declaration of Independence; Paul Revere, the patriotic mechanic; Peter Faneuil, the donor of the market-house and hall that bear his name; Judge Samuel Sewall; six famous doctors of divinity; the first mayor of Boston; and a great many others of whom every student of American history has read. Upon the front of one of the tombs, on the side next to Park Street Church, is a small white marble slab with the inscription, "No. 16. Tomb of Hancock," which is all that marks the resting-place of the famous first signer of the Declaration of Independence, and the first Governor of Massachusetts under the Constitution. In another part of the yard is the grave of the great Revolutionary patriot and Governor of the Commonwealth, Samuel Adams. Near the Tremont House corner of the burying-ground are the graves of the victims of the Boston Massacre of 1770. The most conspicuous monument is that erected in 1827 over the grave where repose the parents of Benjamin Franklin; it contains the epitaph composed by the great man, who, "in filial regard to their memory, placed this stone." Even the briefest reference to the notable persons who lie buried here would extend this sketch unduly.

ENTRANCE TO THE GRANARY BURYING-GROUND.

The row of once stately and beautiful, but now mutilated, elms, outside this burying-ground, has also a history. They were imported from England, and after having been for a time in a nursery at Milton, were set out here by Captain Adino Paddock, from whom the mall now takes its name, in or about 1762. Paddock was a loyalist, and a leader of the party in Boston. He left town with the

British troops in 1776, removed to Halifax, and thence went to England ; but upon receiving a government appointment in the Island of Jersey, he removed thither, and lived there until his death, in 1807. He was a carriage-builder, and his shop stood opposite the row of trees which he planted and cared for. The elms were carefully protected during the occupation of the town by the British. Until within a few years their right to cast a grateful shade upon the throng of pedestrians constantly passing and repassing on Tremont Street has been respected. But three of them have already been sacrificed to false ideas of utility, and on two occasions only the strongest remonstrances of the press and of private citizens have been able to preserve them from the "march of improvement." Some large limbs have been broken off by high winds, others have been amputated in the most uncalled-for manner ; so that in winter the trees are anything but an ornament, though in summer the graceful and abundant foliage conceals the mutilation to which they have been subjected.

The large open spaces in this part of the city have made it a desirable section for residences. It is but lately that business has driven almost all the inhabitants of houses on the easterly side of Tremont Street to remove elsewhere in Boston. The other streets that bound the public grounds have not been invaded. Boylston, Arlington, Park, and Beacon Streets are still among the favorite streets in the city for dwelling-houses. The last-named street is, perhaps, the greatest favorite of all, especially upon the hill opposite the Common, and upon the water side below Charles Street. Near the top of the hill, on this street, stood, until a few years ago, the Hancock mansion, one of the most famous of the old buildings of Boston that have been compelled to make way for modern improvements. This house was in itself and in its surroundings one of the most elegant mansions in the city, though the style of architecture had wholly gone out of fashion long before it was taken down. It was built by Thomas Hancock in 1737, and was inherited by Governor John Hancock. Both uncle and nephew were exceedingly hospitable, and were accustomed to entertain the Governor and Council and other distinguished guests annually on "Artillery Election Day" ; and it is said that every Governor of Massachusetts under the Constitution, until the demolition, was entertained once at least within this mansion. The house was taken down in 1863, and on the site now stand two of the finest freestone-front houses in the city.

THE OLD HANCOCK HOUSE.

Not far away, on the corner of Beacon and Park Streets, is the spacious mansion of the late George Ticknor. This house was erected many years ago, and was at first designed to be very much larger than it was subsequently when occupied. The original owner erected the corner house and the two adjoining dwelling-houses on Beacon Street as a single residence, but the plan was afterwards changed, and what was originally intended for one dwelling-house became three, all of ample size. Mr. Ticknor bought the corner house of the late Harrison Gray Otis, and began to reside there about the year 1830; and it was his Boston home until his death in 1870.

On the slope of the hill, nearly opposite the foot of the Common, stands the dwelling-house occupied by Mr. Ticknor's friend, the historian Prescott, during the last fourteen years of his life. It is unpretentious in architecture, but it was fitted within in a style of great elegance, and was arranged specially with reference to Mr. Prescott's infirmity of blindness. In it the greater part of the work upon his famous histories of the various Spanish conquests was done. To this house he removed, in 1845, from his former home in Bedford Street, and in it he died in 1859.

MR. PRESCOTT'S RESIDENCE, BEACON STREET.

Our space does not admit of a full account of the filling in of the Back Bay lands, — that great improvement by which hundreds of acres have been added to the territorial extent of Boston and millions of dollars put into the State treasury. A few facts and dates only can be given. Private enterprise had already suggested this great improvement when the State first asserted its right to a part of the flats in 1852. The owners of land fronting on the water had claimed and exercised the right to fill in to low-water mark. In this way the Neck, south of Dover Street, had been very greatly widened. Commissioners were appointed in 1852 to adjust and decide all questions relating to the rights of claimants of flats, and to devise a plan of improvement. Progress was necessarily slow where so many interests were involved, but at last all disputes were settled, and the filling was begun in good earnest. No appropriation has ever been made for work to be done on the Commonwealth's flats; the bills have been more than paid from the very start by the sales of land. By the last report of the commissioners it appears that, up to the first of January of the present year (1872), the proceeds of sales have reached the sum of $3,591,514.82, and the total expenses have been $1,547,220.40, leaving more than two million dollars net profit to the Commonwealth. About half a million feet of land still remain unsold, and it is expected that a million and a half of dollars clear profit will be realized from it. This is altogether independent of the land filled by the Boston Water Power Company, and by other corporations and individual owners. It was originally intended that there should be in the district

COMMONWEALTH AVENUE.

filled by the State a sheet of water, to be called Silver Lake, but the idea was subsequently abandoned. A very wide avenue was, however, laid out through it, to be in the nature of a park, and the plan is in process of being carried out. When completed, Commonwealth Avenue will be a mile and a half in length, with a width of two hundred and forty feet between the houses on each side. Through the centre runs a long park in which rows of trees have been planted, and these will, in time, make this avenue one of the most beautiful parks in the country. There are wide driveways on either side; and the terms of sale compel the maintenance of an open space between each house and the ample sidewalks. In the centre of the park, near Arlington Street, stands the granite statue of Alexander Hamilton, presented to the city in 1865 by Thomas Lee, Esq., who subsequently erected, at his own expense, the "Ether Monument" in the Public Garden, before mentioned. Beacon Street has been extended to the Brookline boundary, and a very large part of the land filled and sold by the Commonwealth, between Beacon and Boylston Streets, has been built upon. The nomenclature of the streets in this territory is ingenious, and far preferable to the lettering and numbering adopted in other cities. To the north of Commonwealth Avenue is Marlborough Street, and to the south Newbury Street, which names were formerly applied to parts of Washington Street, before it was consolidated. The streets running north and south are named alphabetically, alternating three syllables and two, — Arlington, Berkeley, Clarendon, Dartmouth, and so on.

Within the limits of the West End district are many of the finest churches in the city proper, and the movement of the religious societies westward and southward is exhibiting no signs of cessation. Some of the oldest societies in town are preparing to emigrate to the new lands of the Back Bay, as, for instance, the Old South and the Brattle Street Churches. Only a few of the churches in this part of the city, some of them very elegant and costly, can be mentioned here. "The First Church in Boston," Unitarian, claims the first attention, though the building is one of the most recent. Allusion has been made already to the first and second houses of this society, in State and Washington Streets. The site of Joy's Building, near State Street, was used by the Society from 1639 until 1807, when it removed to Chauncy Street, and thence in December, 1868, to the new edifice on the corner of Marlborough and Berkeley Streets. This church was built at a cost of two hundred and seventy-five thousand dollars, and is one of the most beautiful specimens of architecture in Boston. Especially fine are the carriage-porch and the vestibule on the Berkeley Street front. The windows are all of colored glass, and were executed in England. The organ, which is one of the best in the city, was manufactured in Germany by the builders of the Music Hall organ. In every part of the building, within and without, are evidences of excellent taste and judgment, such as can seldom be seen in the churches of this country. The church can seat nearly one thousand persons.

FIRST CHURCH, BERKELEY STREET.

On the corner of Boylston and Arlington Streets stands the first church erected on the Back Bay lands of the Commonwealth. This society, like that of the First Church, is attached to the Unitarian denomination. It is, however, the successor of the first Presbyterian church gathered in Boston. It was established in 1727, and its first place of worship was a barn, somewhat transformed to adapt it to its new use, at the corner of Berry Street and Long Lane, now Channing and Federal Streets. The second house, on the same site, was erected in 1744, and within it met the Convention that ratified the Constitution of the United States on the part of Massachusetts, in 1788. It was from this circumstance that Federal Street received its name. In 1786 the Church had become small in numbers, and by a formal vote it renounced the Presbyterian form and adopted the Congregational system. Having occupied for fifty years the third house on the original site, erected in 1809, the society was compelled, by the invasion of business and the removals of its people, to build the house in which it now worships. During the nearly one hundred and fifty years since the foundation of this society, it has had but six pastors, though there was one interval of ten years when it had no regular pastor. The most noted of this brief list was the Rev. Dr. Channing, who was pastor from 1803 until his death in 1842. The Rev. Ezra S. Gannett was ordained and installed as colleague pastor in 1824, and remained colleague and sole pastor until his melancholy death in August, 1871, in the terrible accident at Revere. The vacancy has not yet been filled. The church on Arlington Street is built of freestone, and is a fine structure, though less ornate in its architecture than many others. Its tower contains an excellent chime of bells.

ARLINGTON STREET CHURCH.

The early settlers of New England were not quite so tolerant towards other creeds than their own as they wished others to be to theirs. This is illustrated by their treatment of the Baptists. The doctrine of that denomination was pronounced "abominable," and those who held it were subject to annoyances without number. In 1665 a church was formed in Charlestown in conformity with the permission of the King's commissioners to all people to worship God as they chose. But as soon as the representatives of the crown were gone the court summoned the members to answer for not attending church. When they pleaded in defence their own "meeting," the court regarded it as an additional aggravation, and fined all the culprits. They refused to pay and were sent to jail, where they remained three years. When at last they petitioned to be released, the former judgment was confirmed, and they were sent back to prison. The persecution continued, and generally with considerable activity, until 1680. Two years before that time the Baptists erected their first meeting-house, and having a well-grounded fear that if their purpose was discovered it would be thwarted, they did not allow it to be known until the building was completed for what object it was intended. Even after it had been occupied the society found the doors nailed up one Sunday morning by the marshal, by the order of the court. However, to-day the Baptist denomination may truly claim to be occupying a building whose spire reaches further towards heaven than that of any other church in the city. There have been fourteen pastors of this church in a little more than two hundred years. The pastorate of the Rev. Dr. Neale, who is yet officiating, has extended over a period of thirty-five years, and is the longest but one on the list. The building on Somerset Street was erected in 1858. It is of brick covered with mastic; the spire is two hundred feet high, and the church itself stands on higher ground than any other in Boston.

SOMERSET STREET, WITH CHURCH.

Between the Common and the Granary Burying-ground stands one of the leading churches of the Trinitarian Congregational denomination. The congregation of Park Street Church was gathered in 1809. It took at once, and has ever since maintained, a prominent position among the churches of the city. Its pastors have been able and popular preachers, and few churches in Boston or elsewhere are so uniformly crowded with eager and attentive listeners. The present pastor, the Rev. W. H. H. Murray, who was installed in 1868, is widely known, not only as a brilliant preacher, but as the author of several volumes of sermons and an excellent, though enthusiastic, hand-book on the Adirondack Mountains, and as a popular lecturer. Under his ministrations the point of the old designation of Park Street Church—Brimstone Corner—has been wholly lost.

The history of the society known as the Central Church is brief. The congregation was gathered in 1835 to worship in the Odeon, under the name of the Franklin Church. In May, 1841, the corner-stone of a new church was laid on Winter Street, and the edifice having been completed, was dedicated on the last day of the same year, the society having a week previously assumed its present name. The transformation of Winter Street into a great centre of retail trade compelled the abandonment of the church on this site, and in the fall of 1867 the present elegant house, which had been several years in building, was dedicated. It is built of Roxbury stone with sandstone trimmings, and cost, including the land, upwards of three hundred and twenty-five thousand dollars. A heavy debt, which for some time oppressed the society in consequence of this enormous expenditure, has, within a year or two, been paid in full. The great gale of September, 1869, blew over one of the pinnacles of the spire, which is the tallest in the city, upon the main building, and caused serious damage, which required several months to repair. The interior of this church, notwithstanding an excess of color, is remarkably beautiful.

PARK STREET CHURCH.

The Public Library of Boston is one of the most beneficent institutions that has been conceived by its public-spirited and liberal citizens. The immense library, which has been collected in the short space of twenty years, is valuable not only from the variety, excellence, and number of volumes it contains, but from its accessibility. It is absolutely open to all, and no assessment, direct or indirect, is levied upon those who make use of its privileges. It is conducted, too, on the most liberal principles. If a purchasable book not in the library is asked for, it is ordered at once; and the inquirer for it is notified when it is received. Although the idea of a free public library had been entertained much earlier, it was not until 1852

CENTRAL CHURCH, BERKELEY STREET.

that this institution was actually established. Very soon after the board of trustees was organized, Joshua Bates, Esq., a native of Massachusetts, but at that time a merchant of London, gave to the city the sum of fifty thousand dollars, the income of which he desired should be expended in the purchase of books. The upper hall of the library building has been named Bates Hall in compliment to him. Generous donations and bequests by many wealthy and large-hearted men and women have swelled the permanent fund of the Public Library to one hundred thousand dollars. The city, too, makes liberal annual appropriations both for the purchase of books and periodicals, and for the payment of salaries and other expenses. The total payments from the city treasury on account of this institution and its East Boston branch, during the year ending April 30, 1872, amounted to $74,925. The number of books added during the last year, was 13,708, and of pamphlets, 10,637, making a total at the date of the last Report of 192,958 books, and 100,383 pamphlets. The circulation during the previous year amounted to 380,343 separate issues. The Boston Public Library is thus the first in the country in the number of issues, although it is exceeded in the number of volumes by the Library of Congress. The library, which has been in its present quarters only a little more than fifteen years, has nearly outgrown the capacity of the building, and various devices have to be resorted to in order to accommodate the large numbers of new volumes added annually. In 1871 the library of Spanish and Portuguese books and manuscripts belonging to the late George Ticknor, Esq., were added to the library in accordance with his will. This alone added more than 4,000 volumes and manuscripts to the library, and to provide for future accessions it was determined to remodel the interior to some extent. This work has been performed during the past year, and, when wholly completed, the capacity of Bates Hall, which was before only 200,000, will be increased to 350,000. The expense of these alterations has been about $56,000. Alterations are also contemplated to increase the capacity of the Lower Hall (popular department) of the Central Library. On the 1st of May a new branch was opened in South Boston,

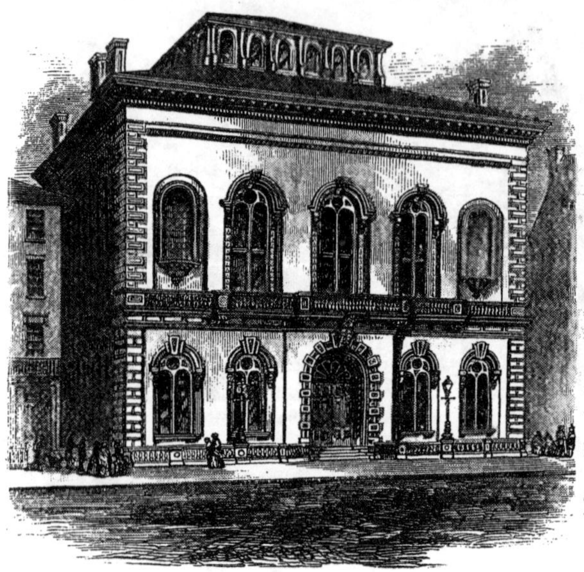

BOSTON PUBLIC LIBRARY.

and a building is now going up in Roxbury, in which a large branch for that section of the city will be opened in the coming winter.

The building of the Boston Athenæum, situated on Beacon Street, not far from the head of Park Street, is an elegant structure, built of freestone, in the later Italian style of architecture. The corner-stone was laid in April, 1847, and the building, which cost nearly $200,000, was occupied in 1849. Within it is a library, now containing nearly 100,000 volumes; a reading-room and an art gallery. The scientific library of the American Academy of Arts and Sciences, of which Benjamin Franklin was once a member, is also kept in the eastern room of the lower floor. The Athenæum had its origin in a magazine called the "Monthly Anthology," which was first published in 1803. Soon after, an association of men zealous for literature was organized, and took the name of the Anthology Club. A public library and reading-room established by this club was the nucleus of the Boston Athenæum, which was incorporated by the Legislature under that name in 1807. The first library room was in Congress Street, but the quarters having become too contracted, Mr. James Perkins, in 1821, conveyed to the Athenæum his own mansion in Pearl Street, — an exceedingly valuable gift, — and the society, having removed thither, remained there until the completion of the new building in Beacon Street. The Athenæum is not a public institution. The right to use the library is confined to the holders (and their families) of about one thousand shares, of whom only about six hundred pay the annual assessment that entitles them to take books from the library. The management is, however, very liberal towards strangers, and the attendants are unremitting in their attentions to visitors. There is an absence of "red tape" in the general direction of the library that not only makes it one of the most delightful literary homes to be found anywhere, but proves that nothing is lost by trusting to

BOSTON ATHENÆUM.

the good taste and sense of propriety of those who resort thither. The gallery of art contains a fine collection of paintings, many of them by famous artists, to which the general public is admitted on the payment of a small fee. It is expected that this collection will be transferred to the projected museum of art, when it has been more fully organized, and thereafter the whole building will be given up to the library and reading-room. The funds of the Athenæum, of which the income is applicable to the uses of the institution, now amount to more than a quarter of a million dollars, beside the real estate and the library, paintings, and statuary, which are valued at upwards of $400,000. Last year there were added to the library upwards of 3,000 volumes at a cost of nearly $7,500, in which, however, was included the expense of periodicals subscribed for, binding, etc.

On the lot bounded by Berkeley, Newbury, Clarendon, and Boylston Streets stand two more of the semi-public institutions of Boston, and both connected with the practical education of the people. Nearest to Berkeley Street on the right of our view is the building of the Boston Society of Natural History, incorporated in 1831. The early days of the society formed a period of constant struggle for existence, from lack of the necessary funds. But the munificence of several citizens, — one of whom, Dr. William J. Walker, gave, during his life and in his will, sums amounting in the aggregate to nearly two hundred thousand dollars, — and the grant of the land on which the building stands, by the State, in 1861, have raised it from its poverty, and given it a position of great usefulness and a reasonable degree of prosperity. The cabinet of this society, which is exceedingly rich in very many branches of natural history, is open to the public for several hours on every Wednesday and Saturday, and this opportunity is made use of by great numbers of citizens and strangers. There is also a fine library connected with the institution, and during the season interesting courses of lectures are delivered.

SOCIETY OF NATURAL HISTORY AND INSTITUTE OF TECHNOLOGY.

The Institute of Technology was founded in 1861 for the purpose of giving instruction in applied science and the industrial arts. The published plan of the institution declares it to be "devoted to the practical arts and sciences," with a triple organization as a society of arts, a museum or conservatory of arts, and a school of industrial science and art. The land for the purpose was given by the State, and the Institute receives one third of the grant made by Congress to the State for the purpose of establishing a college of agriculture and the mechanic arts. The museum already collected includes photographs, prints, drawings, and casts, to illustrate architecture; models of various kinds to give practical instruction in geometry, mechanics, and building; machinery of many patterns to illustrate mechanical movements; models of mining machinery, and a great variety of other useful articles. The school provides six courses of study, in mechanical engineering, in civil and topographical engineering, in chemistry, in geology and mining engineering, in building and architecture, and in science and literature. By the last published catalogue, there were 264 students from thirteen States of the Union and five foreign countries. Degrees and diplomas are conferred on the graduates, according to the course or courses of study pursued. The institution is doing a work of great usefulness. The building is an elegant structure of pressed brick with freestone trimmings. It is one hundred and fifty feet long, one hundred feet wide, and eighty-five feet high. The basement floor is devoted to chemistry and its applications; the first floor contains the officers' rooms, several lecture-rooms, laboratories and museums; in the second story are five lecture-rooms and a great hall, ninety-five by sixty-five feet; and above are other lecture-rooms, museums, studies for the professors, and another large hall. It is intended to erect another building for the museum of the Institute.

VIEW OF PARK STREET.

The Union Club of Boston was founded in the year 1863, for "the encouragement and dissemination of patriotic sentiment and opinion," and the condition of membership was "unqualified loyalty to the Constitution and the Union of the United States, and unwavering support of the Federal Government in efforts for the suppression of the Rebellion." Its organization is continued to promote social intercourse, and to afford the conveniences of a club-house. A spacious private mansion, formerly the residence of the late Abbott Lawrence, on Park Street, was remodelled internally to fit it for the latter use. The membership, which is limited to six hundred, includes many of the best and wealthiest citizens of Boston. It has at present no political character, however, and the condition of membership quoted above has been removed. Our sketch gives a view of Park Street, with the residence of the late George Ticknor and the Union Club House in the foreground.

The Somerset Club was organized in the year 1852, having grown out of another organization known as the Tremont Club, and is now, as it has always been since it took its present name, a club for purely social purposes. The membership has heretofore been limited to two hundred and fifty, but has lately been increased to four hundred and fifty, and will soon reach the limit, recently fixed, of six hundred. The Somerset Club occupied until the present season the elegant mansion at the corner of Somerset and Beacon Streets; but a year or two ago it purchased the magnificent granite front mansion on Beacon Street, represented in the accompanying sketch. This house was built by the late David Sears, Esq., for a private residence. The club found it necessary to make little alteration in the arrangement of the rooms, but it has thoroughly refitted and furnished them, and added other buildings.

BEACON STREET. — THE SOMERSET CLUB.

The Charles River basin, enclosed between Beacon and Charles Streets and the bridge to Cambridge, has long been a favorite course for boat-racing. Uponit are held the regattas provided by the city for the entertainment of the people on the Fourth of July, and private regattas at other times. At the head of the course is situated the Union Boat-Club House, an attractive structure, in the Swiss style of architecture, having a water frontage of eighty-two feet and commanding a fine view of the river. The gymnasium, club committee, dressing and bathing rooms, are especially adapted to comfort and convenience, and superior boating accommodations are provided for the members. The club was organized May 26, 1851, and, with perhaps one exception, is the oldest boating organization in the country. The present building was completed July 3, 1870. The Union had the honor of introducing on the Charles the style of rowing without a coxswain, and in September, 1853, rowed a race at Hull in which, for the first time in the United States, the boat was steered over the course by the bow oar. They were also instrumental in getting up the first wherry race on the river, July 4, 1854, won by the then coxswain of the club. In 1857, the Unions were at the height of their glory, and in June of that year won from the "Harvards" the celebrated Beacon cup, the most beautiful prize ever offered in Massachusetts for such a race. Champion cups, colors, oars, and medals, are among the trophies of the members, won principally previous to the Rebellion, to which date the supremacy of the Charles was held by the Union. Since the construction of the new house the club has rapidly gained in numbers, and now has one hundred and thirty active members.

UNION BOAT-CLUB, CHARLES RIVER.

The Boston and Providence Railroad has for many years occupied for station purposes the building which is represented by our sketch. It has answered reasonably well the necessities of the road, but it had already begun to be too small to accommodate the growing business, when the company was compelled by other circumstances to take action looking to the erection of a new station. The fine thoroughfare known as Columbus Avenue was projected to run directly over the land occupied by this station and to terminate in Park Square. It was impossible to continue the street northerly beyond Berkeley Street until it was settled that it was to be opened through. The negotiations between the railroad company and the city were protracted, but they came at last to a happy issue, and it was decided in the latter part of 1871 that the present station should be removed, and Columbus Avenue extended through to the square. The city paid the large sum of $436,000 for the property necessary to carry out this project. The new station, which is already erecting, is to occupy land to the north-west of the present site. It will be about eight hundred feet in length. The head-house will be in the Gothic style of architecture, of brick, trimmed with two shades of sandstone. The track-house will have a span of one hundred and twenty-five feet, and will be seven hundred feet in length. It will cover five tracks. The design of this new station is admirable, and when completed, at an estimated cost of $600,000, it will be in every way suited to meet the great and growing demands upon the company. Among the "conveniences" in this station will be flower, cigar, theatre-ticket, and periodical stands, waiting and dressing rooms of ample size, a refreshment-room, a barber's-shop, and a billiard-room. As soon as the track-house has been completed the present station building will be abandoned. The Providence Railroad has an excellent local business, serving a great number of the towns in Norfolk and Bristol Counties by its main line and branches; and it also forms part of the popular Shore Line to New York. Alone of all the Boston railroads it did not increase either local or through charges during or after the war, and though this policy involved a temporary loss it has more than justified the far-sighted wisdom that dictated it.

PROVIDENCE RAILROAD STATION.

In the immediate vicinity of the Providence station is the tract known as the Church Street district, where one of the most beneficial enterprises the city has ever undertaken has been carried out within a few years. The district was low, marshy, and unhealthy, but it was covered with permanent buildings. The city undertook to raise the whole district, and this it did at an expense of about a million dollars. In the course of this operation nearly three hundred brick buildings were raised, some of them fourteen feet, and the whole territory was filled in to a uniform height. A similar process has been going on for some time in the "Suffolk Street district," and is now nearly completed.

On the corner of Beacon and Tremont Streets stands the Tremont House, a hotel that has for a long time enjoyed a deserved reputation for the excellence of its accommodations and its *cuisine.* This house received President Johnson as a guest when he visited Boston on the occasion of the dedication of the Masonic Temple in June, 1867. Its front is imposing, though plain and devoid of ornamentation. Most of the leading hotels of Boston are in close proximity to the centre of business, and this is especially true of the Tremont. Like them, it has lately been undergoing extensive improvements, of which the most notable is the reconstruction of a part of the basement into a beautiful and finely furnished *café.* The Tremont House was originally built by a company of gentlemen, but it was, in 1859, purchased for the Sears estate, of which it now forms a part. The Tremont and Revere Houses are both under the same efficient management.

TREMONT HOUSE.

VIEW AT THE HEAD OF STATE STREET.

IV. THE CENTRAL DISTRICT.

WE come now to a district smaller than either of those that have been described, but one that is much more compact and more crowded. It has already been remarked that the physical characteristics of Boston determined the limits within which mercantile business could have free and natural expansion. The singular and unexplained movements of business, which, nevertheless, have their almost invariable rules, have given the North End up for the most part to retail establishments. In the immediate neighborhood of the wharves some branches of wholesale trade still flourish ; and in the neighborhood of Faneuil Hall there are large establishments for the supply of household stores and furnishing goods of various descriptions ; and there are very few districts in the city which have not retail supply stores of all kinds in their immediate neighborhood. But in general it may be said that the district bounded by State, Court, Tremont, Boylston, and Essex Streets is the business section of the city. State Street is the head-quarters of bankers and brokers, — the money centre of the city. Pearl Street is the greatest boot and shoe market in the world ; and it is curious that, with the exception of a restaurant for boot and shoe dealers, a newspaper devoted to the boot and shoe trade, and other establishments as intimately connected with the business, there are no buildings on the street not occupied by merchants in this special line of trade. On Franklin, Chauncy, Summer, and other streets in the neighborhood, are the great establishments that make Boston the leading market of the country for American dry-goods. Boston also stands first among American cities in its receipts and sales of wool, and the dealers in this staple are clustered within the district we have circumscribed. The wholesale merchants in iron, in groceries, in clothing, in paper, in fancy goods and stationery, in books and pictures, in music and musical instruments, in jewelry, in tea, coffee, spices, tobacco, wines and liquors, — in fact, in all the articles that are necessities or luxuries of our modern civilized life, — have their places of business within it. The retail trade, too, is domiciled here, convenient of access to dwellers in the city and shoppers from the suburbs. The army of lawyers is within the district, or just upon its borders. The great transportation companies have their offices here, supplemented by the express companies that perform the same business upon a more limited, and yet, in another sense, upon a more extended scale. Most of the daily papers are congregated in the immediate vicinity of their advertising patrons. And finally, the people come to this part of the city not only to obtain the every-day articles of use, but to listen to lectures, to applaud at musical concerts, to weep and smile over dramatic representations. By day and by night it is thronged, not by the inhabitants of the district, for very few residents have been able to withstand the onset of business, but by the dwellers in other cities and towns and in other parts of Boston.

Much that is interesting in Boston's history has occurred in this part of the city, but very few of the buildings that are reminders of events long past remain. Even

VIEW OF FRANKLIN STREET.

Fort Hill, one of the historical three, has been wholly removed, and the broad plain where it once stood is now available for building purposes. The earth thus removed was used in carrying forward two other great improvements, —the one to enlarge the facilities for rapid and economical transaction of business ; the other to convert a low, swampy, and unhealthy neighborhood into a dry and well-drained district, — the grading of the marginal Atlantic Avenue and the raising of the Suffolk Street district. Some of the old landmarks yet remain, and, it is to be hoped, will long be permitted to remain as links between the present and the past.

Although this is pre-eminently the business section of the city, it contains several public and semi-public buildings which perhaps deserve the first attention. And the list should properly be headed by the magnificent City Hall, which is one of the most imposing and perfect specimens of architecture in the city. It has been said already that Faneuil Hall was occupied for town purposes from the time of its erection until after the constitution of the city government. It was in 1830 that the city offices were removed to the Old State House, which had been remodelled for the purpose. But only a few years elapsed before it became absolutely necessary to remove thence. Successive city governments having refused to sanction the erection of a suitable City Hall, as recommended by nearly every mayor, the old Court House, which stood on a part of the site of the present City Hall, was converted into a city building in 1840, and all the offices of the city were removed thither. This was, however, but a temporary expedient, and the old difficulties began to arise again, with increased vexation to the crowded officers and the unfortunate public. In 1850 the question of making additions to the old City Hall or of erecting a new one reappeared in the city council; and the records show that from that time hardly a year passed without a recommendation of decided action by the mayor, and an abortive attempt in the city council to pass an order for carrying that recommendation into effect, until a beginning was finally made by the passage of the necessary orders in 1862. The sum originally asked for and appropriated was $160,000. The committee which reported the plan expressed the belief "that the building as proposed can be erected of suitable materials," for this sum, "if contracted for during the present year." The value of estimates is shown by the fact, that the building actually cost, before it was occupied, more than half a million dollars, of which less than seventy-five thousand dollars were paid for work not included in the original estimate. However, the people of Boston long ago ceased to complain of the unexpectedly large addition to what they had been at first asked to invest in a city building.

CITY HALL.

The corner-stone was laid on the 22d of December, 1862, — the anniversary of the landing of the Pilgrims at Plymouth. The building was completed and dedicated on the 18th of September, 1865. The tablet in the wall back of the first landing perpetuates in beautifully worked marble the statement that the dedication took place on the 17th of September. That day would have been highly appropriate for the ceremony, being the two hundred and thirty-fifth anniversary of the settlement of Boston, had it not fallen on Sunday. The ceremony was accordingly postponed until the following day.

The style in which this building has been erected is the Italian Renaissance, with modifications and elaborations suggested by modern French architects. The material of the exterior is the finest Concord granite. The interior is equally as perfect in its arrangement as is the exterior in its beauty and richness. The Louvre dome, which is surmounted by an American eagle and a flagstaff, is occupied within by some of the most important offices of the city. Here is the central point of the fire-alarm telegraphs. An alarm from the most distant part of the city is communicated instantaneously to the watchful operator, who is on duty day and night; and almost before the nervous hand of him who gave the alarm has done its work, the bells in all parts of the city are tolling out the number of the district in which a fire has been discovered, and the engines summoned to extinguish it are proceeding at full speed toward it. All the officers of the city have commodious and comfortable quarters within the building; and although the city council had an eye from the first to the possibility that the building would by and by need to be enlarged to accommodate the city government when Boston should have grown in importance and wealth and population, there has been as yet little inconvenience or crowding, even since the absorption of Roxbury and Dorchester.

CUSTOM-HOUSE.

In the lawn in front of the City Hall stands the bronze statue of Benjamin Franklin, which was formally inaugurated, with much pomp and ceremony, on the 17th of September, 1856. It originated in a suggestion made by the Hon. Robert C. Winthrop, in an address before the Massachusetts Charitable Mechanic Association in 1852. The association took up the matter with enthusiasm, and was joined by a large number of citizens. A public subscription to the amount of nearly

$20,000 furnished the means. The artist was Mr. R. S. Greenough, who was born almost within sight of the Boston State House, and all the work from beginning to end was done in the State. The statue is eight feet in height, and stands upon a pedestal of verd antique marble, resting on a base of Quincy granite. In the die are four sunken panels, in which are placed bronze medallions, each representing an important event in the life of the great Bostonian to whose memory the statue was raised.

The Custom House, on State Street, was begun in 1837, two years after it had been authorized by Congress, and was twelve years in building. It is in the form of a Greek cross, and the exterior is in the pure Doric style of architecture. The walls, columns, and even the entire roof, are of granite. The massive columns, which entirely surround the building, are thirty-two in number. Each of them is five feet two inches in diameter and thirty-two feet high, and weighs about forty-two tons. The building rests upon about three thousand piles. It is supposed to be entirely fireproof, and it is so undoubtedly from without. It cost upwards of a million dollars, including the site and the foundations. President Jackson signed the resolution authorizing its erection; but President Polk's term had been nearly completed when the new Custom House was first opened. It has already become somewhat dingy within, and is attractive only after the spring and fall cleaning and whitewashing.

On the 16th of October, 1871, was laid the corner-stone of what will be, when completed, the finest public building in New England. Our sketch shows what the new Post-Office is designed to be. It has a front of over two hundred feet on Devonshire Street, occupying the whole square between Milk and Water Streets. The following description of the architect's design was printed in the newspapers, on the occasion of the laying of the corner-stone: "A noble basement or street story of twenty-eight feet in height, formed by a composition of pilasters and columns resting on heavy plinths or pedestals of the sidewalk level, and crowned with an entablature, carries two stories above it, both of which are enriched by ornate windows, and dressings admirably in keeping with the best examples of the style selected. The principal entablature of the exterior walls will be singularly effective in detail, upon which will be seated one of the most conspicuous roofs yet introduced in any structure, public or private, erected in this country. In the several faces of the street sides of this roof are to be placed highly burnished dormer windows, intended to be constructed of stone or iron, above which the top of the roof will be finished with cornice and facia, forming the seating of the bronze grille, intended to enclose the entire upper section or flat of the roof. In idealizing the roof of the structure, the architect has introduced several exceedingly novel and expressive features of finish, avoiding, it is believed, the sameness of expression which too often characterizes the 'Louvre' and 'Mansard' roofs. The Devonshire Street façade will be subdivided into five compartments by a 'central projection' flanked by two 'curtains,' finishing at the corners of Water and Milk with 'pavilions.' The 'central projection' and the two pavilions will be respectively subdivided in their height by orders of pilasters, columns, entablatures, and balustrades, and the curtain finish is to be dependent for its effect upon the window dressing and attached entablatures and balustrades, excepting in the first or street story, where the order of the first or

THE NEW POST-OFFICE.

street story before referred to is to be carried uniformly through the entire length of the three street façades. The principal central entrance in the Devonshire Street façade communicates with a broad staircase, located in a noble hall, communicating directly with the second, third, and fourth stories. The remaining entrances of this side of the building give access to the Post-Office corridor, twelve feet in height, above which the strong light to be secured by the liberal window openings of the first story will insure the full lighting of the Post-Office apartment behind the corridors of this and the other two streets on which the building bounds. Both the corner pavilions of the Devonshire Street side are repeated on the Milk and Water Street sides, and the architecture of these last will correspond, in detail and finish, with the Devonshire Street front aforesaid. Two groups of statuary are designed in the central projection of the Devonshire Street side, — one of them to crown the principal entrance, and the other group to surmount the fine stone 'attic' which covers the central projection, and faces the more elevated portion of the roof over that side of the structure. The central group of statuary, on the attic, is to be flanked by sculptured eagles, respectively located over the two outer corners of the attic."

When the "corner-stone" was laid, the edifice had already been nearly finished to the top of the street story; but the occasion was a favorable one for a street parade, and the presence of the President of the United States and several members of his Cabinet added to the interest of the ceremonies. The Boston Post-Office has been somewhat of a migratory institution. During the siege of Boston it was removed to Cambridge, but was brought back again after the evacuation of the town by the British. In the last ninety-six years it has been removed at least eight times. For the last eleven years it has been without interruption in the Merchants' Exchange Building in State Street, but the present is its third occupation of the same quarters. The government has never owned the building in which the Boston Post-Office has been located. In the magnificent structure now building the upper stories will be occupied by the sub-treasury, which at present has its quarters in the Merchants' Exchange Building over the Post-Office. The new building has already been in process of erection more than two years, and it will probably be two years more before it will be wholly finished, although a much earlier occupation of the Post-Office quarters is contemplated. When completed, it will have cost more than two million dollars. At present the avenues of approach to this building are neither numerous nor broad, but plans have been prepared for several street widenings that will, if they are carried out, make these important public offices easily accessible from all the business centres of the city.

The County Court House in Court Square was erected in 1833, and is a substantial but plain and gloomy-looking building. There has been for some time past a movement in favor of a new court-house. Thus far there has been no agreement as to a suitable site, and no decisive step has been taken for a removal from the present inconvenient building and noisy neighborhood. The United States Courts occupy the building at the corner of Temple Place and Tremont Street, — a structure of very fine appearance and well suited to its present use. This building was erected in 1830 by the Freemasons of Massachusetts as a Masonic temple, but it was subsequently used as warerooms for Chickering's pianos, and finally it was purchased by the United States government and fitted up as a court-house. Its architecture is quite unique. The walls are of Quincy granite cut into triangular blocks. The effect is not unpleasant, but it is surprising that the Masons of all

ST. PAUL'S CHURCH AND THE UNITED STATES COURT-HOUSE.

others should have departed from their established rule of "square work." With its two massive towers, its long arched windows, and its sombre general aspect, the suggestion of the building is rather that of a church than of a court-house.

Our view also includes a sketch of St. Paul's Episcopal Church, adjoining the Court-House. The society worshipping in this church was formed in 1819, and the corner-stone was laid on the 4th of September of that year. The edifice was completed, and consecrated by the bishops of Massachusetts and Connecticut on the 30th of June, 1820. It has since been extensively remodelled in the interior. The walls of this church are of a fine gray granite, but the Ionic columns in front are of Potomac sandstone laid in courses. This church is at present without a rector, the Rev. Dr. Nicholson having recently resigned, and his place not being yet filled.

Two of the oldest church buildings in the city are left within this district, surrounded by business structures and far from the dwelling-houses of the worshippers who meet within their walls. The Old South Society was the third Congregational Society in Boston, and was organized in 1669, in consequence of a curious theological quarrel in the First Church. The first church building of this society, erected in 1669, stood for sixty years. It was of cedar, and it had a steeple and galleries, with the pulpit on the north side. It was taken down in 1729, when the present building was erected on the same spot, and religious services were held in it for the first time on the 26th of April, 1730 (O. S.). This meeting-house is perhaps the most noted church edifice in the United States. It is internally very quaint and interesting. Its sounding-board over the pulpit, its high, square box-pews, its double tier of galleries, in fact its whole appearance, attract the visitor's attention, and lead him to inquire into its history if he does not already know it. But a tablet high above the entrance on the Washington Street side of the tower gives concisely the main facts. The Old South is frequently mentioned on the pages devoted to the history of Boston before and during the Revolution. When the meetings of citizens became too large to be accommodated in Faneuil Hall, then much smaller than now, they adjourned to this church. Here Joseph Warren stood and delivered his fearless oration, on the anniversary of the massacre of March 5, 1770, in defiance of the threats of those in authority, and in the presence of a marshalled soldiery. Here were held the series of meetings that culminated in the destruction of the detested tea, on

OLD SOUTH CHURCH.

which the determined colonists would pay no tax. In 1775, the British soldiers, eager to insult those by whom they were so cordially hated, but whom they held so completely in their power, occupied this meeting-house as a riding-school, and place for cavalry drill. They established a grog-shop in the lower gallery, which they partially preserved for spectators of their sport. The rest of the galleries were torn down, and the whole interior was stripped of its woodwork. The floor they covered with about two feet of dirt. At this time the church was without a pastor, and no new pastor was ordained until 1779. In 1782 the building was thoroughly repaired and put in very much its present condition. The first Election sermon was delivered in the Old South Church in 1712, and the ancient custom is still observed. As soon as the two branches of the Legislature have met and organized, the Governor is notified that the General Court "is ready to attend Divine service," the procession is formed, and the State government marches to this historic building to hear a sermon by a preacher designated by the preceding Legislature. But this ancient church must give way to the march of business. Its members live at a distance, and they are to abandon the spot consecrated by the memories of more than two centuries for a new meeting-house on land reclaimed from the sea.

King's Chapel, too, standing at the corner of School and Tremont Streets, has its history, hardly less interesting than that of the Old South. It is, as is well known, the successor of the first Episcopalian church in Boston. There were a few of the early settlers in the town, who belonged to the Church of England. Very timidly did they ask in 1646 for liberty to establish their form of worship here, "till inconveniences hereby be found prejudicial to the churches and Colony." Very decidedly were they rebuffed, and no more was heard of the matter for many years. The Church of England service was, however, introduced by the Chaplain to the commissioners from Charles II. in 1665, and from that time there was little hindrance to their forms.

KING'S CHAPEL.

Nevertheless, it was not until twelve years after this that a church was actually formed, and not until 1686 that steps were taken to erect a building to accommodate it. Governor Andros in that year greatly offended the consciences of the Old South people by determining to occupy the Old South for an Episcopal church, and by compelling them to yield to him in this matter, though very much against their will. However, about that time, the church was built on a part of the lot where stands the present building. It is not possible to ascertain how the land was procured for the purpose; and some have believed that Andros appropriated it in the exercise of the supreme power over the soil which he claimed by virtue of the delegated authority of the King. However, the church was built there, and by the middle of July, 1689, it was occupied. In 1710 the building was enlarged, but by the middle of the century it had fallen to decay, and it was voted to rebuild with stone. The present building was first used for Divine service August 21, 1754. During the British occupation of the town it was left unharmed. Not only was this the first Episcopal church in Boston, it was also the first Unitarian church. While the Old South Meeting-house was undergoing repairs of the injuries sustained in its occupation as a military riding-school, the society of King's Chapel gave to the former society the free use of the Stone Church. When the Old South people returned to their own house, the proprietors of King's Chapel voted to return to their old form of worship, with extensive alterations in the liturgy, adapting the Church of England service to the Unitarian doctrine.

Adjoining this ancient church is the first burial-ground established in Boston. It is not exactly known when it was first devoted to the burial of the dead. There is some dispute over the question whether Mr. Isaac Johnson, one of the most prominent of the colonists, and also one of the first to pass away, was or was not buried here. It is, however, certain that this was the only graveyard in Boston for the first thirty years after the settlement. The visitor to this yard will be apt to notice the very singular arrangement of gravestones alongside the paths. They were taken from their original positions years ago, by a city officer, who was certainly gifted with originality, and reset, without the slightest reference to their former uses or positions, as edgestones or fences to the paths. Notwithstanding this not very praiseworthy improvement, which leads one to wonder how much further it was carried, there are still many very old gravestones in this yard. Three, at least, date back to the year 1658. One of these stones has a history. At some time after the interment of the good deacon it commemorated, the stone was removed and lost; but it was discovered in 1830 near the Old State House, several feet below the surface of State Street. It is of green stone, and bears this inscription:—

HERE : LYETH
THE : BODY : OF : MR
WILLIAM : PADDY : AGED
58 YEARS : DEPARTED
THIS : LIFE : AUGUST : THE [28]
1658.

On the reverse is this singular stanza of poetry: —

HEAR . SLEAPS . THAT
BLESED . ONE . WHOES . LIEF
GOD . HELP . VS . ALL . TO . LIVE
THAT . SO . WHEN . TIEM . SHALL . BE
THAT . WE . THIS . WORLD . MUST . LIUE
WE . EVER . MAY . BE . HAPPY
WITH . BLESSED . WILLIAM PADDY.

A great many distinguished men of the early time were buried in this enclosure, and several of the tombs and headstones still bear the ancient inscriptions. The tomb of the Winthrops contains the ashes of Governor John Winthrop, and of his son and grandson, who were governors of Connecticut. All three, however, died in Boston, and were buried in the same tomb. Not far away is a tablet supported by four upright posts, from which we learn that "here lyes intombed the bodyes" of four "famous reverend and learned pastors of the first church of Christ in Boston," namely, John Cotton, John Davenport, John Oxenbridge, and Thomas Bridge. This burying-ground has not been used for interments for a very long time. It is occasionally opened to visitors, and well repays a visit, though all the inscriptions on all the tombs and stones were long ago copied and published.

Tremont Temple is one of the best known halls in the city for public assemblies of all kinds. It stands on Tremont Street, directly opposite the Tremont House, on the site of the old Tremont Theatre. It covers more than 12,000 square feet of ground. The front of Tremont Temple is covered with mastic, and is seventy-five feet high. Within is the great audience-room, one hundred and twenty-four feet long, seventy-two feet wide, and fifty feet high, with its deep, encircling galleries. It was in this hall that Mr. Charles Dickens gave his readings in Boston on his last visit to America, and it was selected on account of its great capacity and admirable acoustic properties. The hall is very plain indeed. Even the organ, which often adds so much to the appearance of halls and churches, is merely hidden behind a screen, and is without a case. The Temple is occupied on Sundays by the Tremont Street Baptist Church for its services. The Young Men's Christian Association has its quarters

TREMONT TEMPLE.

in this building, and there is, beneath the Temple proper, a smaller temple, — the Meionian. From the cupola of the building, which is, however, not very accessible, a fine view of Boston and the surrounding country is to be had.

Standing on Tremont Street, at the head of Hamilton Place, and looking down the place, one may see a plain and lofty brick wall without ornament or architectural pretensions of any sort. The building is the Boston Music Hall, one of the noblest public halls in the world, and the pride of every music-lover of Boston. This hall was built by private enterprise, and first opened to the public in 1852. It has ever since been the head-quarters of musical entertainment in the city. It would require more space than can be devoted to the subject to give even a list of the great singers whose voices have been heard within its walls, of the famous lecturers who have expounded their views here, and of the numerous fairs for charitable purposes that have been held in it. But it is safe to say that in no other single hall in the country have so many and so choice programmes of music been performed, and that no other hall has furnished a platform for so many distinguished orators during the past twenty years. The acoustic properties of the hall are perfect. Indeed, it is, as Dr. Holmes has well said, "a kind of passive musical instrument, or at least a sounding-board constructed on theoretical principles." It is one hundred and thirty feet in length, seventy-eight in breadth, and sixty-five in height. The height is half of the length, and the breadth is six-tenths of the length, the unit being thirteen feet. No one who has been inside the hall needs to be told of its architectural beauty, its spaciousness, its entire suitability to the purpose for which it was designed. The brilliant light shed down from the hundreds of gas-jets encircling the wall far above the upper balcony is something to be remembered. The fine statue of Apollo, the admirable casts presented by Miss Charlotte Cushman and placed in the walls, and above all the magnificent statue of Beethoven, by Crawford, standing in

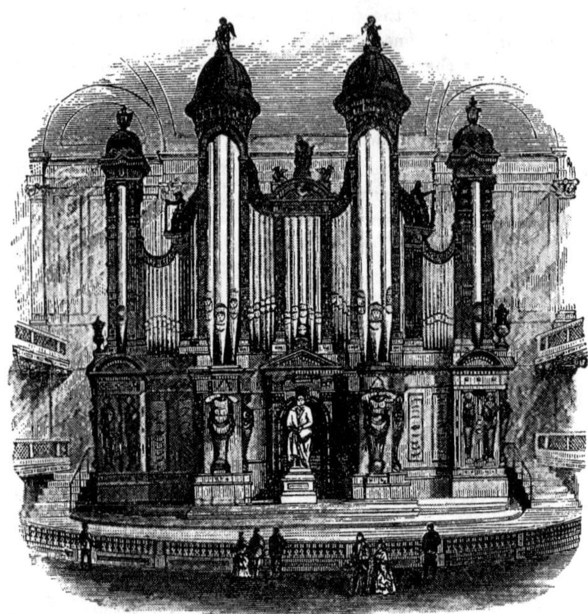

THE ORGAN IN MUSIC HALL.

front of the organ, deserve the attention of every visitor to the hall. But all these works of art are speedily forgotten in the presence of the glorious instrument that is the chief ornament and attraction of the Music Hall. The organ was contracted for in 1856, with Herr E. Fr. Walcker of Ludwigsburg, Wurtemberg, and was set up and formally inaugurated on the 2d of November, 1863, in the presence of an immense and delighted audience. Hundreds of thousands of people have since listened to its grand and beautiful tones. The organ contains five thousand four hundred and seventy-four pipes, of which no less than six hundred and ninety are in the pedal organ; and it has eighty-four complete registers. Its architecture is exceedingly rich and appropriate, and a close inspection is necessary to reveal the beauties of which only the general effect can be here reproduced. Only those who have been inside the great instrument know how complete and thorough was the work. Even the brass pipes that imitate the trumpet are shaped like the orchestral trumpet, and are of polished brass; and the series of flutes are of choice wood, turned and varnished, fashioned like actual flutes, and fitted with *embouchures* of brass. It is in all its parts the most perfect, as it is on the whole the largest, organ in the country. The whole cost of the organ and its case was upwards of $ 60,000.

The Boston Museum, near the head of Tremont Street, is one of the oldest of the places of amusement in Boston. In 1841, Mr. Moses Kimball and associates opened the "Boston Museum and Gallery of Fine Arts," in a building erected for the purpose at the corner of Tremont and Bromfield Sts. In connection with the museum, it had a fine music-hall, capable of seating twelve hundred people, where the drama very soon found a home. The success of the venture was so great that the present building was erected in 1846, and the first entertainment was given in it on the 2d of November in that year. The museum proper is very large and interesting. It occupies numerous alcoves in the large hall on Tremont Street, the hall being furnished with several capacious galleries, which are all filled with curiosities and works of art. The theatre is large and well

BOSTON MUSEUM.

ventilated, comfortably furnished and finely decorated. It is managed with liberal shrewdness. The "star" system is wholly discarded, and the dramas are represented by an excellent stock company. The veteran William Warren, who became connected with this theatre the second season, and has been a member of the company every year but one since, is a host in himself. Several other actors and actresses have been at the Museum so long that they would hardly be at home on any other stage. This theatre is a very great favorite with all classes of patrons of the drama. It used to be called the "Orthodox theatre" on account of the distinction made by some good people who objected to dramatic entertainment in general, but saw no harm in attending the representation of plays at the Museum. The Museum is now under the administration of Mr. R. M. Field, who has occupied the position of manager for nearly eight years.

The Boston Theatre is situated on the west side of Washington Street, between Avery and West Streets. It is the largest regular place of amusement in New England, and is in many respects one of the finest. The opportunity for architectural display was most limited, and no hint whatever is given of the lofty and spacious auditorium by the external appearance of the entrance. This theatre is owned by a stock company, but is managed by private enterprise. It was erected in 1854, and was opened on the 11th of September of that year, under the management of Mr. Thomas Barry. There is a stock company connected with this theatre, but there is almost always a "star" performer to attract the multitude, — and a very large multitude can be accommodated within it. This is the house usually engaged for the representation of Italian, German, and English Opera. Most of the great American actors, and many distinguished foreign actors and actresses, have appeared upon this stage. Jefferson and Owens, Booth and Forrest, Fechter and Sothern, Ristori and Janauschek, and a host of

others whose names are famous in the annals of the stage, have here delighted the Boston public within the last five years alone; while of opera-singers may be mentioned Nilsson, and Parepa Rosa, and Kellogg, and Phillipps. The Boston Theatre is now under the management of Mr. J. B. Booth.

The Globe Theatre is the newest and one of the most attractive of the theatres of Boston. It was built in 1867 by Messrs. Arthur Cheney and Dexter H. Follett, and opened in October of that year as Selwyn's Theatre, Mr. John H. Selwyn being the manager. After three years of successful management Mr. Selwyn retired, and was succeeded by Mr. Charles Fechter, who had, a few months before, carried Boston by storm by his acting at the Boston Theatre. Mr. Fechter's managerial experience in Boston was brief, and he, in turn, gave way to Mr. W. R. Floyd, who is now the manager. Mr. Cheney meanwhile had become the sole owner of the theatre. The name of the house was changed to the Globe on the retirement of Mr. Selwyn. The decoration of the auditorium is remarkably tasteful and brilliant. Although very rich colors are employed, the harmony and complementary appropriateness of each to the other are so perfect that there is no approach to gaudiness. The stage appointments have always been unexceptionable under the several managements; so that while one is listening to the words of the play, the eye, as well as the ear, is gratified. Under Mr. Selwyn the theatre was managed upon the stock-company principle; Mr. Fechter was his own star; and under Mr. Floyd there has been a combination of both systems. Mr. Charles Mathews, Mr. John E. Owens, Miss Charlotte Cushman, and Miss Carlotta LeClercq may be mentioned among others who have played star engagements during the last two years. In common with all the regular theatres of Boston, it has enjoyed a very high and uniform degree of prosperity.

Freemasonry has long been in a very flourishing condition in Boston, and, indeed,

MASONIC TEMPLE.

in Massachusetts. After the political excitement against the order, thirty or forty years ago, had died out, there was a reaction in its favor, and since that time it has had hardly a check to its progress. The fine building now used for the United States courts was used as the head-quarters of the order until the limits were outgrown. Subsequently the several organizations, or a large number of them, were gathered in the building adjoining the Winthrop House, at the corner of Tremont and Boylston Streets. Both the hotel and the halls were destroyed by fire on the night of April 7, 1864. It was then determined to build a temple worthy of the order on the same site. The corner-stone was laid with imposing ceremonies on the 14th of October of the same year, and the temple, having been wholly completed, was dedicated on the Freemasons' anniversary, St. John's Day, June 22, 1867. On the latter occasion President Johnson was present, having accepted an invitation to participate in the ceremonies, which drew together delegations of brethren of the order from all parts of Massachusetts and New England. The building is of very fine granite, and has a front of eighty-five feet on Tremont Street. Its height is ninety feet, though one of the octagonal towers rises to the height of one hundred and twenty-one feet. It has seven stories above the basement, of which only the street floor is occupied for other than masonic purposes. There are three large halls for meetings on the second, fourth, and sixth floors,

finished respectively in the Corinthian, Egyptian, and Gothic styles. On the intermediate floors are anterooms, small halls, and offices; while in the seventh story are three large banqueting-halls. Both in its external appearance and in its internal arrangements this temple is a credit to the order and an ornament to the city.

Within the limits of the district we have described are, as we have said, most of the daily newspapers and most of the weeklies. Several of the former are established permanently in buildings erected specially for their use. The Boston Post occupies the building at the corner of Water and Devonshire Streets, opposite the new Post-Office, except the second and third floors, which are let out for business purposes. The first number of the Post was issued on the 9th of November, 1831, by Charles G. Greene. In that first number the editor promised "to exclude from its columns everything of a vindictive or bitter character," and although he announced his intention to discuss public questions freely and fearlessly, he agreed to do so "in a manner that, if it failed to convince, should not offend." The promise has been faithfully kept. The Post has frequently maintained the unpopular side in political controversies, but it has always done so without offensive pertinacity or personal diatribes, and thus it has managed to have almost as many friends among those opposed to it in opinion as among those of its own political faith. It has also always maintained a reputation for liveliness and cheerful humor that has been well deserved, and has stood it in good stead. The Post was first published in the present commodious quarters on the morning of March 29, 1869. Its counting-room is on the street floor, its press-room in the basement, the editorial and reporters' rooms on the fourth floor, and the composing-room on the fifth.

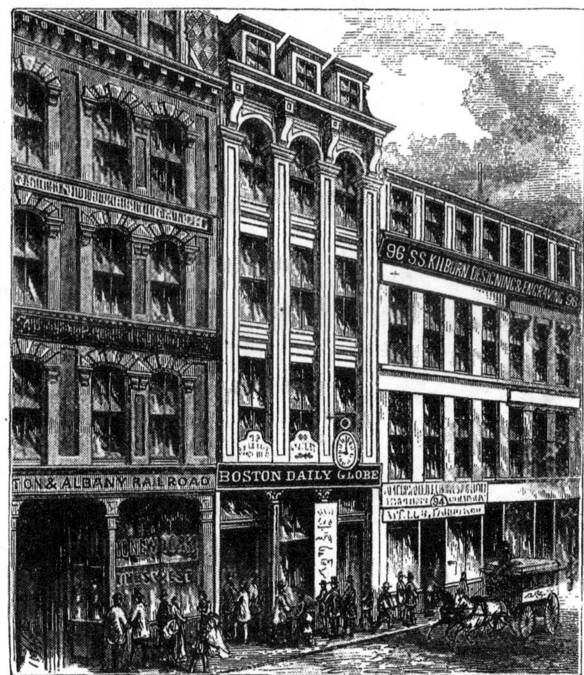

VIEW IN WASHINGTON STREET : GLOBE OFFICE.

The only other strictly morning paper to be noticed is the Globe. This is the latest venture in journalism in Boston. It was a long time in planning, and was not issued until every preparation had been made. The building it occupies is that but recently vacated by the Transcript, and is well suited to the present use. The Globe was first published on the morning of March 4, 1872. It is a quarto sheet, and the only Boston daily that takes that form regularly. It is independent in politics. It aims to give a large amount of news, — local, national, and foreign, and has thus far had a greater degree of success than could have been anticipated when it was originally projected. Its circulation is said to be quite unusual for a newspaper so recently started, and it has already become a worthy rival to its longer established neighbors.

The Transcript was the pioneer of the evening press in Boston, and is, next to the Advertiser, the oldest daily newspaper in the city. It was first published in July, 1830, and the senior partner of the original firm is still the head of the house. The experiment was for some time one of doubtful success, but it grew in popularity, and now no paper in Boston is more firmly established. During the more than forty years since its first publication it has had but four editors-in-chief, of whom the present editor is now in the twentieth year of his service. The Transcript has always been a pleasant, chatty, tea-table paper, full of fresh news, literary gossip, and choice extracts from whatever in any branch of literature was new and entertaining. It aims to please the Boston public, and has never made any strenuous exertions to extend its circulation far beyond the city's limits, and yet it is highly esteemed abroad. The building in which it is now permanently established is a fine granite-front structure four stories in height, with a double French roof above. As with most of the other newspapers occupying their own buildings, the basement and street floor are reserved for press-room and counting-room, the second and third floors are let for business purposes, and the two upper floors are reserved for editorial and composing rooms.

VIEW IN WASHINGTON STREET: TRANSCRIPT OFFICE.

The Evening Traveller occupies a building at the corner of State and Congress Streets, — quarters in which it has been established since 1854. The Daily Traveller was first issued on the 1st of April, 1845, as a two-cent evening paper, — the first in Boston to adopt a price so low. The weekly American Traveller had then been issued more than twenty years, having been first published in January, 1825. In its day the American Traveller was the great paper for stage-coaches and steamboats. When the daily was founded, it adopted a course quite different from that of any other paper in Boston. It aimed to be a moral and religious organ as well as a medium of news. The old traditions are still retained to some extent in the Traveller, but it long ago adopted the purveyance of news as its leading object. In this particular its reputation is firmly established, the news department, under a liberal management, being always fresh and well arranged. The arrangement of the Traveller office is similar to that of the other offices that have been mentioned, with one or two exceptions. The great value of space in State Street has led the Traveller to share its counting-room with others. One corner of the room is occupied by a telegraph-office, and in the two corners on State Street are located, in rather narrow quarters, two brokerage-houses; and above, on the fourth floor, are to be found both the composition and editorial rooms. A view of the Traveller building is given in the illustration of State Street.

VIEW IN WASHINGTON STREET.

The Boston Journal is both a morning and an evening paper. The second and third pages always contain the latest news, in whatever edition it is sought. The Journal long ago obtained an excellent reputation as a general newspaper, both for the counting-room and the family circle. It has a very large sale throughout Massachusetts, Maine, and New Hampshire, and in consequence of the peculiar character of its constituency has always been especially strong in its New England intelligence. The Journal was founded in 1833, appearing for the first time on February 5 of that year as the Evening Mercantile Journal. On beginning the publication of a morning edition, it took its present name. The Journal was the first newspaper in Boston to procure a Hoe press. It now uses two, — one of six cylinders, and the other of eight. The present building was occupied in September, 1860. Its arrangement is similar to that of other papers already described.

The Boston Herald is also a morning and evening paper, and enjoys a very great popularity. It was first issued in 1846 as a one-cent paper, and this price it maintained until the general rise of prices during the war. The Herald circulates a very large number of copies, its daily issue being exceeded by only one or two newspapers in the country. It is the only one of the Boston papers that has yet adopted the practice of stereotyping its "forms," and this course it was compelled to adopt by the impossibility of printing the requisite number of copies in the time at its disposal. The Herald is also the only daily of those already named that publishes a Sunday issue.

In addition to the newspapers mentioned there are two other dailies, — the Times, an evening paper, and the News, published morning and evening, and sold for two cents each; the Times, like the Herald, publishing a Sunday issue. There are also many other weekly newspapers, weekly, political, religious, agricultural, pictorial, and literary, many of them with very large circulation, and conducted with marked ability. There are no less than five Sunday papers, a number that is hardly exceeded by any city in the country. And there is probably no other business that has experienced a more uninterrupted prosperity for the past ten years, or that has resulted in more satisfactory returns to the pockets of the investors, than the business of newspaper publishing in Boston.

The fine hall of the Massachusetts Charitable Mechanic Association stands upon the northwest corner of Bedford and Chauncy Streets. This association, of which Paul Revere was the first president, had been agitating the question of erecting a hall for more than half a century before the steps were finally taken that resulted in the building of this structure. The land was bought in December, 1856, for

MECHANICS' BUILDING.

$31,000. It fronts ninety-three feet on Chauncy Street, and sixty-five feet on Bedford Street. The building was immediately begun upon a plan designed by Hammatt Billings, and it was completed and dedicated in March, 1860, at a cost, including land, of about $320,000. It is constructed of dark freestone in a modification of the Italian Renaissance style of architecture. During the erection of the City Hall the building was occupied by the offices of the city government. The large hall and the accompanying rooms on the second floor are now used by the Boston Board of Trade and the National Board of Trade.

A fine piece of architecture is the Horticultural Hall, on Tremont Street, between Bromfield Street and Montgomery Place. It was erected by the Massachusetts

HORTICULTURAL HALL AND STUDIO BUILDING.

Horticultural Society, and is one of the most perfectly classical buildings in the city. It is built of fine-grained white granite, beautifully dressed, and the exterior is massive and elegant in proportion. The front is surmounted by a granite statue of Ceres. The lower floor is occupied for business purposes, and above are two halls, not very large, yet adapted not only to their original purpose, for the meetings and exhibitions of the society, but for parlor concerts, lectures, social gatherings, and fairs. The series of Sunday afternoon lectures delivered in this building during each winter for several years past have made Horticultural Hall almost as well known in this country as Exeter Hall is in England. On the opposite corner of Bromfield Street stands the Studio Building. This structure is occupied on the street floor by six large stores, while above is a perfect hive of artists. This building, indeed, is the head-quarters of the artists of Boston, though many of them are located elsewhere. There are delightful artists' receptions here, to which the general public is invited. Besides the devotees of art, there are many private teachers of music and the languages in the Studio Building, and not a few of the rooms are occupied as bachelors' apartments.

The building occupied by the Mason & Hamlin Cabinet Organ Company for their warerooms on Tremont Street is a marble structure of great architectural beauty, which has added not a little to the attractiveness of Tremont Street, and has aided in drawing business down that avenue below Temple Place. It was begun in the spring of 1866, and was completed in the following spring, at a cost of about $175,000. The Mason and Hamlin Company is more extensively engaged in manufacturing reed musical instruments than any other establishment in the world. It has turned out upwards of sixty thousand instruments in the eighteen years since the business was begun, and the business has increased three-fold in the last seven years. The company is now exporting many instruments of its manufacture to Europe. It has two extensive manufactories, one on Cambridge Street, Boston, and the other in Cambridge.

VIEW IN TREMONT STREET.

At the corner of Washington Street and Central Court is the elegant building occupied by Jordan, Marsh, & Co. as a retail dry-goods store. It has a fine front of dark freestone, eighty feet long on Washington Street and five stories high. The street floor and basement only were at first occupied by the firm. The second floor was used as a wareroom by Chickering & Sons, the rear being finished off into a beautiful hall, while the upper floors were let to lodgers. The whole building is now occupied by the firm, and the wholesale department has been removed from Devonshire Street to a new building in the rear. The two structures cover a surface of from 20,000 to 23,000 square feet, and are connected by an excavated passage-way. Each building is furnished with a passenger and a freight elevator, all of them operated by a stationary engine in the passage-way between the two buildings.

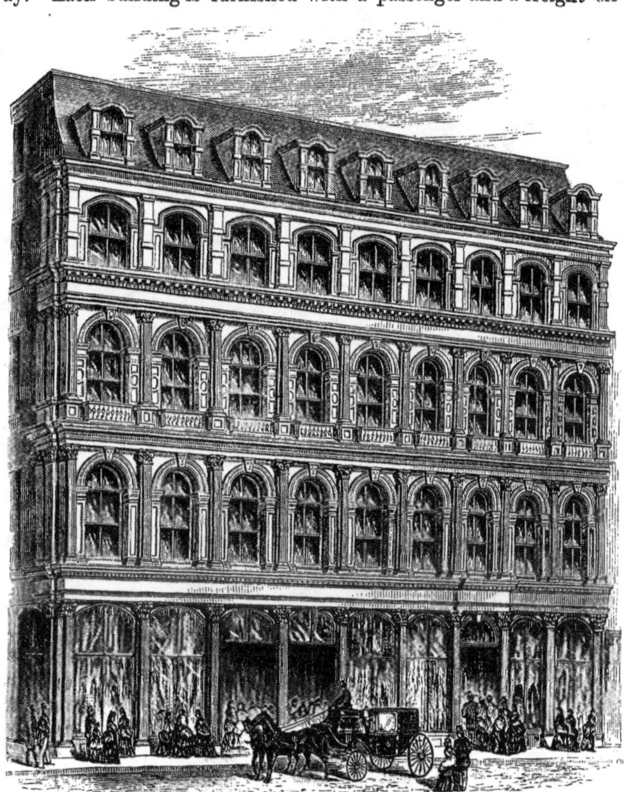

JORDAN, MARSH, AND CO.'S BUILDING.

The Old Corner Bookstore, now occupied by Messrs. A. Williams & Co., is one of the very oldest buildings now standing in the city. The exact date of its erection is not known, but the building which preceded it on the same site was destroyed by the great fire of October, 1711, and in a short time, probably within a year, the Old Corner Store was erected. The history of this store has been very carefully and completely traced from its first occupation as an apothecary's shop, by the builder, Mr. Thomas Crease, to its reversion to the original use in 1817. In 1828 Messrs. Carter and Hendee took it for a bookstore, and to that use it has ever since been devoted. Four years after the date just mentioned, Messrs. Allen and Ticknor, the lineal ancestors of the present house of James R. Osgood & Co., took this position, and retained it under the successive management of William D. Ticknor, Ticknor, Reed, & Fields, and Ticknor & Fields, until 1865, when the last-named firm removed to the quarters on Tremont Street now occupied by their successors. The Old Corner Store combines excellence of situation

OLD CORNER BOOKSTORE.

with a sort of rambling picturesqueness that has made it a great favorite with lovers of books. It has been preserved in very nearly its original form, and will probably be permitted to remain for many years as one of the best and most substantial examples of a style of architecture that has gone wholly out of vogue.

The present quarters of the publishing-house of James R. Osgood & Co., successors to Ticknor & Fields and Fields, Osgood, & Co., are in the first of a row of buildings that reach from Hamilton Place to Winter Street, on Tremont Street. A generation ago these fine granite-front structures were among the most elegant private mansions in the city. One by one they have been given up to business until all are now so occupied. Their size and arrangement made them admirably adapted for transformation into stores. The publishing-house occupies the entire building. From this house are issued four periodicals, — the North American Review, the Atlantic Monthly, Our Young Folks, and Every Saturday. This house retains all the impor-

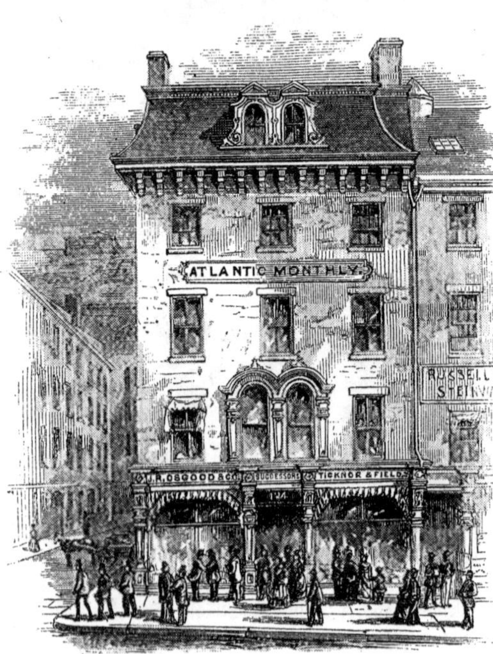

tant literary relations and the valuable copyrights which have been acquired during forty years under its various names. Among its authors are Longfellow, Whittier, Emerson, Hawthorne, Lowell, Holmes, Mrs. Stowe, Tennyson, Dickens, Thackeray, and many other of the first authors of America and England.

The magnificent marble structure on Washington Street occupied by Macullar, Williams, & Parker, for their great wholesale and retail clothing manufactory and salesroom, was built by the trustees of the Sears estate. Its fine marble front cannot fail to attract notice, and its internal arrangements are as perfect as its architecture. It was built especially for this firm, and was arranged to suit them. At the time it was erected it was the largest building in the world wholly devoted to the business of clothing manufacture, and perhaps it is so now. It fronts only forty feet on Washington Street, but it extends back to Hawley Street two hundred and fifty feet, and is five stories in height. There is in every room an abundance of light and air, and the State Board of Health made a special note of the regard paid in these respects by this establishment to the health of the men and women employed.

MACULLAR, WILLIAMS, AND PARKER'S BUILDING.

The Sears Building, on the corner of Court and Washington Streets, is one of the finest, as it was also for its size one of the costliest, business structures in the city. The land was bought and the work of tearing down the old buildings was begun in June, 1868. The foundation was laid in July, and within a year the new building was occupied. It has a front of fifty-five feet on Washington Street, and of one hundred and forty-nine feet on Court Street. It is built in the Italian-Gothic style of architecture, the external walls being constructed of gray and white marble, the contrast of which is highly pleasing. The price paid for the land on which this building stands was $356,000, which was at the rate of about forty-three dollars a square foot, and the building itself brought the entire cost of the property up to about three quarters of a million dollars. It is furnished within in a style of great elegance, and is occupied by two banks, several insurance companies, a score or more of railroad companies, engineers, treasurers of companies, etc. A steam elevator of the best and latest pattern is kept constantly running, to convey passengers from the street floor to the top of the building. This elegant structure appears on the right of the large view on page 50 of this book.

The crookedness of Washington Street is not in all respects a disadvantage. It permits many fine buildings to be seen to better advantage than they would be if the street had been laid out in a straight line. In passing along the street, one of the most prominent buildings, and one of the most recent additions to the fine architecture of the street, is the banking-house of the Mercantile Savings Institution. This is, however, an old building with a new front, and otherwise reconstructed. The new front is of veined marble, resting on three columns of highly polished red Quincy granite. The elegant steps which give access to the basement and the first story are of pure white marble. Within, the apartment of the bank, which occupies the whole of the first story, is finished in black walnut, the walls are tastefully frescoed, and the floors and counters are of marble.

Artemus Ward, in a saying which has become proverbial, located Harvard College in the billiard-room of Parker's, on School Street. But it is not with the Harvard students alone that the Parker House is a favorite. Charles Dickens, who had, of course, a predilection for a hotel on the European plan, gave it the name of being the best house at which he had been a guest in America. The proprietors of the Parker House began in a small way in another building, and gained a reputation for providing the best that the market afforded, which they have never suffered themselves to lose. Their present quarters are elegant externally, and sumptuously furnished within. The house is patronized very extensively by persons travelling for pleasure, and is a universal favorite with visitors as well as citizens. Its prosperity is so great that the proprietors have found it necessary to make an addition of two stories to their present building, and to purchase an estate on Tremont Street, which will give the hotel a much-needed entrance from that thronged avenue. This new addition will consist of a six-story marble building of fine architectural appearance.

We end this chapter as we began it, with a view in State Street. This time our sketch shows the magnificent row of warehouses at the lower end of State Street, known as State Street Block, which contains some of the most substantially built and commodious stores in Boston. The former proprietors having filled in the dock between Long and Central Wharves, and having driven about eight thousand piles, began to lay the foundations of this structure in December, 1856. The lots were sold by auction in June, 1857, one of the terms of the sale being that the purchaser should erect upon the lot bought a building in accordance with a specified plan, so as to make the entire block uniform. The lots brought prices ranging from $18.75 down to $5.37½ per superficial foot. The building, or rather the collection of buildings, erected, covers an area 425 feet long on State and Central Streets, and is of a uniform depth of 125 feet. The walls are laid in rough granite ashlar. The stores have each five stories and a double attic above the street, and the height of the buildings from the street to the crown of the roof is about 92 feet. The general appearance of this block of fifteen stores is of extreme solidity and of complete adaptation to the purpose for which they were designed. Many other wharves in Boston besides Long Wharf are covered with solid and capacious warehouses, though this State Street Block is the largest and most elegant of all. The visitor in the city will find agreeable occupation for many a leisure hour in wandering about the wharves, where there is, under the revival of commerce in Boston, a perpetual scene of activity. The most important wharves in Boston proper are those in the immediate vicinity of State Street, — especially Central, India, and T Wharves, where most of the large steamers in the coasting trade arrive, and whence they depart. Atlantic Avenue, which is rapidly becoming an important channel of communication between the several wharves, passes directly across the foreground of our view of State Street Block.

THE PARKER HOUSE.

STATE STREET BLOCK.

The retail trade of the Central District of Boston is chiefly transacted in that section bounded on the east by Washington Street, the greater part of the territory between Washington Street and the wharves being given up to wholesale business. The ladies' quarter has its centre at the corner of Washington and Winter Sts. On any pleasant day the sidewalks and stores in the immediate vicinity of that corner are crowded with ladies engaged in the delightful occupation of "shopping," and the streets are lined with their carriages. The railroads have made it possible for the inhabitants of the cities and towns of half Massachusetts to make their ordinary purchases in Boston, and the large proportion of ladies carrying little travelling-bags is an indication of the extent to which advantage is taken of the possibility.

V. THE SOUTH END.

THE South End of Boston, as the term is now understood, is a district of residences. It is true that Washington Street, throughout its whole length, is given up almost entirely to retail trade, and that a considerable amount of business is done on other streets. There are too, here and there, large manufactories that are not to be overlooked. But, generally speaking, Boylston Street divides the business of the city on the north from the residences on the south. It is impossible to predict how long this state of things will continue. Boston business is rapidly expanding, and the room to do it in must expand likewise. The current is setting decidedly to the south, and year by year new advances are made in that direction, by both wholesale and retail trade. It is the firm belief of many that Columbus Avenue will ultimately become a great retail business street, but that is looking far into the future. Yet it can have escaped no one's observation, that the district between Boylston Street and the Albany Railroad is in the state of transition that invariably precedes the full occupation of a position by trade. But we must speak of the existing lines of division; and for our purposes we regard as the South End, given up to residences, all the territory bounded on the north and west by Essex, Boylston, and Tremont Streets, and the Boston and Albany Railroad, and south by the old Roxbury line.

VIEW IN CHESTER SQUARE.

The face of the country in this part of the city is for the most part level; and indeed a very large part of the territory was reclaimed from the sea. A great number of the horse-cars run to the "Neck," but the South End is no longer a neck of land. There are many among us who remember when Tremont Street was but a shell road

VIEW OF BOSTON FROM TREMONT STREET NEAR CHESTER PARK.

across flats. Now it is a spacious avenue lined with imposing structures, as may be seen in our large view. Only a few public spaces were reserved in this part of the city. Franklin and Blackstone Squares are merely open spaces, — of great value, to be sure, for breathing purposes, but incapable, both from their small size and from their flatness, of being made very beautiful. Union Park, Worcester Square, and Chester Square have been made desirable for residence and for public resort by simple and inexpensive means. The last-named has long been a favorite street for dwelling-houses, many of which are very elegant and costly. Through the avenue runs a park, narrow at the ends, but swelling out in the centre, in which are trees and flowers, with a fountain and a fish-pond, making the park a deliciously cool and pleasant spot in midsummer. Most of the streets, other than those we have named, though generally pleasant, are somewhat monotonous in their appearance. One street, which is not an exception to the rule of monotony, but which is nevertheless a favorite place for residences, is Columbus Avenue. This is one of the longest straight streets in the city. It is laid out in a direct line from West Chester Park to Park Square, but has thus far only been completed to Berkeley Street. It has been paved for the greater part of its length with wood, and this partially explains its popularity, for it is chosen, on account of its even pavement, as a driveway, by great numbers of public and private carriages, making it always a lively street, though never a noisy one. Columbus Avenue ends in a pleasant little square at its junction with West Chester Park, and when it shall have been wholly built up, this will be one of the most delightful spots at the South End.

There are but few public buildings in this section of the city, and we begin by

GIRLS' HIGH AND NORMAL SCHOOL.

giving a view of one that should be characteristic of the district, as well as illustrative of the admirable school buildings for which Boston is celebrated, the last and best school-house provided by the city for the education of youth. The Girls' High and Normal School is built upon a lot fronting 200 feet on West Newton and Pembroke Streets, and 154 feet in depth. The building itself has a front on each street of 144 feet, and a depth of 131 feet. The school has a capacity equal to the accommodation of 1225 pupils. The total cost of the land and the building was $310,717, of which about $60,000 was paid for the land, and $16,000 for the furnishing. It would be impossible within our limits to give even a brief description of this perfect school-house. It has an abundance of rooms for every department of the school, for museums, and collections of all kinds of articles necessary to the instruction here given. There are no less than sixty-six separate apartments, exclusive of halls, passages, and corridors. They are all well lighted and cheerful. The entire building is supplied with hot air, radiated from apparatus located in the cellar, and is ventilated in the most thorough manner. The large hall in the upper story has received, through the generosity of a number of ladies and gentlemen, a large collection of casts of sculpture and statuary. Every room is placed in direct communication with the master's room by means of electric bells and speaking-tubes. On the roof is an octagonal structure, which is designed to be used as an astronomical observatory. In every respect this school-house is suited to the purpose for which it was designed, and is a credit to the city.

WASHINGTON STREET, WITH CONTINENTAL HOTEL.

Within a few years the French "flat" system of dwellings has been very extensively adopted in Boston. There are now as many as twenty great "hotels," as they are called, divided into suites of apartments where families may lodge and "keep house" all on one floor. These suites are of various sizes, and are variously arranged, but the principle is the same. There are, too, very many houses formerly used as single residences, that are now let out to tenants, who take all the rooms on one floor; and again there are "family" hotels, where the apartments are arranged for the most part in suites, but where there are no kitchens, thus obliging the guests to take their meals at a restaurant, or at a *table d'hôte.* But we have now to do with the French system, pure and simple, which is illustrated in the immensely long and commodious Continental Hotel, in the Hotel Berkeley, and the Hotel Boylston. In structures of this class, a family rents a suite of rooms all upon one floor. Each suite has its own front door, — opening into a general hall, to be sure, — with an entry hall, parlor, dining and sleeping rooms, kitchen, etc. It is a house in itself. The tenant is generally relieved of the necessity of buying fuel, the heat being supplied by steam from the basement. Except that he uses the same street-door, the same staircases, and the same hall with his fellow-tenants, he is as isolated from the rest of the world as he would be in a house of his own. The Hotel Pelham, on the corner of Boylston and Tremont Streets, was the first hotel of this kind erected in Boston, but of late the system has become exceedingly popular, and the demand so far exceeds the supply that proprietors are able to ask and to obtain large prices for rent. One of the most elegant of this class of dwelling-houses is the Hotel Boylston, opposite the Hotel Pelham and the Masonic Temple. It has been but recently erected by the Hon. Charles Francis Adams. Its architecture is remarkably pleasing and tasteful, and its location gives it a great advantage over some other fine buildings that must be examined, if at all, from the opposite side of a narrow street. The interior has been arranged with great care to fit it for occupation by families, and its central location, added to its own excellence and elegance, have already made it a great favorite with those who are fortunate enough to have their domicile beneath its roof.

HOTEL BOYLSTON.

Some also of the largest hotels of the old-fashioned sort in the city are within the South End district. We give a sketch of one, — the St. James. It was built by Mr. M. M. Ballou, and opened in April, 1868. Standing as it does upon Newton Street, facing Franklin Square, the beauty of its proportions may be seen to the best advantage. It is elegantly finished and furnished throughout, with all the appliances of a modern hotel, including a passenger elevator worked by steam. The great dining-hall is capable of seating two hundred and fifty people. Some of the rooms in this house are most sumptuously furnished. During the short time it has been open,

ST. JAMES HOTEL.

it has had for guests several distinguished persons, chief among whom is President Grant. Another hotel, and a most elegant one, is the Commonwealth, on Washington Street, between Worcester and Springfield Sts. The material of the fronts on each of these streets is marble, and the hotel is finely finished and furnished throughout.

Among a great number of churches in this part of the city, only a few can be mentioned. Most prominent already, though it is not yet completed, is the Cathedral of the Holy Cross, on Washington and Waltham Streets. The corner-stone of this church was laid in the summer of 1867. An army of workmen has since been engaged upon it at all seasons when building was possible, but it is still far from completion. The great tower at the southwest corner will be 300 feet high, and so immensely high are the walls of the church, and so large is the surface of ground covered by it, that this height is only in strict proportion to the other dimensions of the structure. Already a small chapel — small, however, only in comparison with the rest of the building — has been finished, and its gorgeousness of color and the elegance of the fittings and ornamentation exceed that of any other church in New England. It is promised that even this shall be surpassed by the decoration of the Cathedral itself. It is claimed that

CATHEDRAL OF THE HOLY CROSS.

when the great auditorium shall have been finished, its numerous and wide entrances will permit the exit of a full congregation more rapidly and easily than any other church in Boston. Probably something of the same spirit that led the Old South Society to insert over its church-door a tablet recording the fact that it was "desecrated by British soldiers" during the Revolution, and that led the people of the Brattle Square Church to build the cannon-ball from Bunker Hill into the wall of their edifice, has inspired the Roman Catholics to construct a part of the wall of this cathedral with brick from the ruins of the Ursuline Convent in Somerville. That convent was burned in 1834, and the ruin being at that time a more effective reminder of the popular hostility to the sect than a new convent would be, it was never rebuilt. It is somewhat singular that the Catholics have suffered less in Boston from proscriptive laws and the activity of religionists opposed to them than the Baptists or the Episcopalians. In 1647 a law was passed prohibiting any ecclesiastic ordained by the authority of the Pope or See of Rome from coming into the colony, but there is no evidence that it was ever enforced, or that any one ever suffered in person or property in Massachusetts by the authority of the government exercised against the Roman Catholic faith. In 1788 a Catholic chapel was dedicated. It is probable that services had been held in Boston long before, but neither, then, nor before, nor since, so far as the records show, was any attempt made to suppress them. Contrasted with their lot, the imprisoned and banished Baptists, the proscribed Episcopalians, and the executed Quakers, had a hard time indeed.

Not very far distant from the Cathedral, on Harrison Avenue, are the Church of the Immaculate Conception and Boston College (which is under the auspices of the Catholics), side by side. The church was begun in 1857, and dedicated in 1861.

CHURCH OF THE IMMACULATE CONCEPTION AND BOSTON COLLEGE.

It is a solid structure of granite, without tower or spire. Above the entrance on Harrison Avenue is a statue of the Virgin Mary, with an inscription in Latin, while above all stands a statue of the Saviour, with outstretched arms. The interior of this church is very fine. It is finished mainly in white, except at the altar end, where the ornamentation is exceedingly rich and in very high colors. The organ is regarded as one of the most brilliant in the city. This church has always been noted for the excellence of its music. The college was incorporated in 1863, and has been very successful. The number of students is smaller than in some of the other colleges in the State; still, it is increasing, and the class of young men who here receive higher education is one not reached by the Protestant colleges. The cost of the church and the college buildings was about $350,000.

Among the many Protestant churches in this district of the city, we speak of but one, the Methodist Church, on Tremont Street, between Concord and Worcester. This has long been regarded as one of the finest church edifices in Boston, as it certainly is the finest belonging to the Methodist denomination. It was one of the first, if not the very first, constructed of the Roxbury stone, which has now become so very popular. The plan of the church, with its spires of unequal height at opposite corners, is unique, and the effect is exceedingly pleasing. The society worshipping here was formerly known as the Hedding Church. Meetings were first held at the corner of Shawmut Avenue and Canton Street in 1848. A brick church was built the next year on South William Street, which was occupied until the present edifice was dedicated, on the 1st of January, 1862. The structure is in the plain Gothic style, and stands on a lot 202 feet long and 100 feet in depth. The entire cost of land, buildings, bell, and furniture, was only $68,000. The land alone is worth much more than that sum to-day, and the church could not be replaced, if it were destroyed, for the amount originally paid for the entire estate of the church.

METHODIST CHURCH, TREMONT STREET.

More than twenty years ago the expediency of establishing a City Hospital was mooted. The physicians of the city urged it very strongly, and the subject was much discussed in the City Council. But, like many other projects of the kind, this one was put off from year to year, although the necessity for such an institution was all the time growing greater. At last in 1858 the Legislature gave the city the necessary authority, and in the last days of December, 1860, a lot of land on the South Bay territory, owned by the city, was appropriated for a City Hospital. The work was begun in the fall of 1861, the buildings were dedicated on the 24th of May, 1864, and opened for the reception of patients the following month. The lot of land on which the Hospital stands contains nearly seven acres, occupying the entire square bounded by Concord, Albany, and Springfield Streets, and Harrison Avenue. A large tract of land east of Albany Street is also occupied for hospital purposes.

CITY HOSPITAL.

The Hospital proper consists of a central building for administration, pay-patients, and surgical operating-room; two pavilions connected with the central building by corridors; and another pavilion for separate treatment. The architectural effect, as will be seen from our sketch, is very fine. The Hospital receives and treats patients gratuitously, though many pay for their board, thereby securing separate apartments and additional privileges. During the year ending with the month of April, 1871, there were 2569 patients treated within the Hospital, besides 8899 who were under medical treatment in the department for out-patients. For the support of the inmates of the institution during that year the city paid more than $ 95,000.

The people of the South End have been, until recently, without any general market; but the want has now been supplied. A great market building was erected in 1870 at the corner of Washington and Lenox Streets, and is thus accessible to the people both of the South End and of Roxbury. The building is about two hundred and fifty feet in length, and the lot on which it stands is about one hundred and twenty feet wide. There are nearly one hundred stalls. This is one of the neatest and best kept markets in the city. Its stalls are clean and bright as well as roomy, and the general facilities for doing business here by the market-men from the country, by the occupants of the stores, and by the general public, are of the very best.

On one of the most conspicuous sites at the South End, on the corner of Berkeley and Tremont Streets, stands the now nearly completed Odd Fellows' Hall. It is a building of elegant design and of imposing appearance. The near expiration of the lease of the halls now occupied by the order compelled the Odd Fellows to seek quarters from which they could not be driven. The step was decided upon in January, 1870; the Odd Fellows' Hall Association was incorporated by the Legislature at that time in session, the money was raised, the site purchased, and work was begun immediately. The corner-stone was laid in the summer of 1871, and the exterior of the building was completed before the winter set in. Since then the interior has been receiving constant attention, and the hall will soon be occupied. This structure covers about twelve thousand square feet, and is constructed of Concord and Hallowell white granite. It is four stories in height, of which the first or street story will contain seven large stores, with spacious basements beneath, extending out under the sidewalks. The second story will contain one audience-hall, with convenient anterooms and side-rooms; also six offices on Tremont Street, with entrance from Berkeley

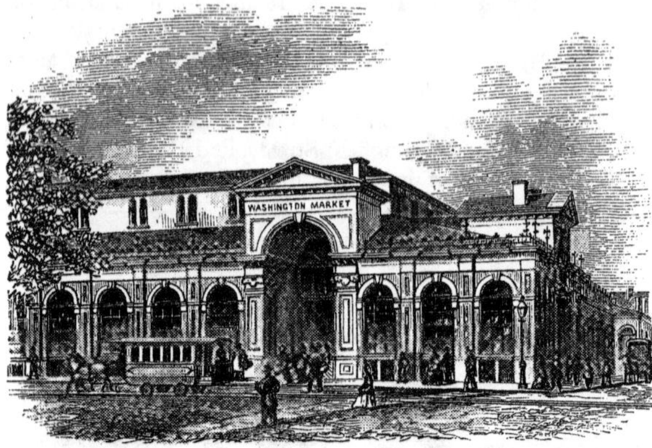

WASHINGTON MARKET.

ODD FELLOWS' BUILDING.

Street. The third story will contain three large working-halls, with suitable anterooms, side-rooms, and closets; also grand lodge office and grand master's private room, with other appendages; also library-room and four committee rooms. The fourth story will have one mammoth hall, fifty-four by ninety-four, and twenty-five feet high in the clear from floor to ceiling, with anterooms and side-rooms; also a banquet-hall, twenty-six by one hundred and ten feet, with adjoining rooms and closets. The roof story will contain the encampment hall and other available rooms. The grand entrance to all these halls will be from Tremont Street.

The Central Club is an organization lately formed. It began in a little circle, holding almost informal meetings at the St. James Hotel, in 1869. The necessity for a social club at the South End had long been felt by many, and this organization rapidly increased in membership. Only a few months after the earliest meetings, rooms were leased on Concord Street; and in the new quarters the Club was once more besieged with applications for admission to membership. Another removal became necessary, and in 1871 the elegant brown-stone residence on the corner of Washington Street and Worcester Square was leased for a term of seven years. The Central Club, having fitted up this building in a manner combining elegance and comfort, removed thither early in the present year (1872). The apartments are spacious, admirably arranged, and richly furnished. From the large cupola, which is reached by a winding staircase, a fine view of the harbor, the Highlands, and the surrounding country, can be obtained.

CENTRAL CLUB.

The passenger station of the most important railroad leading out of Boston, the

Boston and Albany, is situated on Beach Street, between Albany and Lincoln Streets. It is a plain structure of brick, and is neither as commodious, as convenient, nor as comfortable as the business of the company warrants and demands. The company itself is aware of this, and has been for some time contemplating the erection of a larger and better station, but as yet its plans have not been matured. This station is divided longitudinally, so that outward and inward bound trains leave and arrive at two practically distinct stations, —a plan which greatly lessens the confusion usually arising from the meeting of opposing currents of passengers. The Albany road exceeds all the other railroads centring in Boston, not only in length, but in the amount of business done both in passengers and freight. Its supremacy in the latter particular is very marked. The Eastern Railroad presses close upon its heels in the number of passengers carried, but the Albany road transports more merchandise than all the other railroads entering Boston combined. Although others of our railroads have western and southern connections, the Albany has the greater part of the land travel to New York and the South, as well as of the travel to Albany and the West. And it is very much the most important line of transportation of freight, especially of western productions, to Boston.

The Old Colony and Newport Railroad serves the entire South Shore of Massachusetts and Cape Cod; and it also forms a link of one of the most popular railroad and steamboat lines to New York, known as the "Fall River Line." The Old Colony road is about to absorb the Cape Cod Railroad, the Legislature having given the necessary authority, and both roads having voted in favor of the union. The growth of both local and through business on this line during the past few years has been very great, owing to the rapid increase of population along the line and the enterprising management of the company's affairs. The latter fact is illustrated by the encouragement given to new settlers in suburban villages. A year or two ago the company offered a free pass for a term of years to every person who would buy and occupy during that time a house at Wollaston Heights in the town of Quincy. The result of this experiment has been an immense increase in the revenue of the company from that station. Similar liberality on the part of other railroads would doubtless lead to equally gratifying results. The station building of this road, at the corner of Kneeland and South Streets, makes no architectural pretensions externally, but within it is one of the largest and best structures of the kind in the city. Its waiting-rooms and offices are light and airy, and are made as comfortable as the most comfortless of apartments, railroad waiting-rooms, can be.

OLD COLONY RAILROAD STATION.

The United States Hotel, one of the largest hotels in the city, is directly opposite the Albany Station; and being, at the same time, one of the best kept public houses in Boston, and near the centre of business, it has a deservedly large share of the patronage of travellers.

VI. NEW BOSTON AND THE HARBOR.

WE have already said that Boston has grown in territorial extent not only by robbing the sea, but by absorbing other outlying tracts of land and whole municipalities. The first addition of the latter kind was made in 1637, when Noddle's Island was "layd to Boston." It was of very little use to the town, however, for it was practically uninhabited until 1833, when a company of enterprising capitalists bought the entire island and laid it out for improvement. Its growth since that time has been very rapid, and it is still capable of great increase in population, as well as in wealth and business. A part of South Boston was taken from Dorchester in 1804 by the Legislature, much against the will of the people of that town, and annexed to Boston. Again, in 1855, the General Court added to the territory of the city by giving to it that part of South Boston known as Washington Village. However, Boston has now made it all right with Dorchester by taking to itself all that remained of that ancient town. Roxbury, which had a history of its own, and a name which many of the citizens were exceedingly loath to part with, became a part of Boston on the 6th of January, 1868. It was incorporated as a town but a few days after Boston, it was the home of many distinguished men in the annals of Massachusetts and the country, and it took a glorious part in the several struggles in which the Colonies and the Union were engaged. In the old times, when a narrow neck of land was the only connection between Boston and Roxbury, there were good reasons why the two should be under separate governments; but long ago the two cities had met, and joined each other. It was not uncommon for buildings to be standing partly in one city and partly in the other. A man might eat dinner with his wife, he being in Boston, while she, on the opposite side of the table, was in Roxbury. When at last the long-vexed question was submitted to the voters of the two cities, it was enthusiastically decided by both in favor of union. Dorchester was incorporated the same day as Boston. It too had its history, and but for the manifest advantages to both municipalities of a union, might have retained its separate existence. The act of union, passed by the Legislature in June, 1869, was accepted by the voters of both places the same month, and the union was consummated on the 3d of January, 1870. It is with a few among the many objects of interest in these outlying parts of Boston, and in the harbor, that we shall have to do in this chapter.

One of the most interesting of the public institutions in the city is the Perkins Institution and Massachusetts Asylum for the Blind, at South Boston. It has been more than forty years in operation with uninterrupted and most remarkable success. It was instituted in 1831. In the following year, Dr. Samuel G. Howe undertook its organization, and began operations with six blind children as the nucleus of a school. For a year the institution was greatly hampered by a lack of funds; but a promise of an annual grant by the Legislature, a generous sum raised by a ladies' fair, and liberal contributions by the people of Boston, speedily settled the financial question, and opened a period of prosperity and usefulness which has continued to the present time. By the last report of the trustees in September, 1871, it appears that the whole number of inmates since the opening of the Asylum was then 774, and the average number during preceding years was 153. The amount of good done by this Institution during the forty years it has been in operation is incalculable. Wonders have been accomplished in the instruction of unfortunate youth deprived of sight, and in some cases, notably that of Laura Bridgman, the absence of the sense of hearing also has not been an insuperable obstacle to learning. During its whole existence, this asylum for the blind has been under the direction of Dr. Howe, and a great deal of the success of the experiment is to be credited to his peculiar fitness for the position, and to his devotion to its interests. The main building, which is shown by our sketch, is situated on high ground on Mount Washington. Quite recently the plan of the institution has been changed. The sexes are entirely separated, the ladies and girls having been removed to four dwelling-houses built for the purpose. The inmates, of both sexes, are divided into families, each of which keeps a separate account of its expenses. The Asylum is partly self-supporting, such of the pupils as are able to pay maintaining themselves as at a boarding-school, and all the pupils being taught some useful trade. Several States, particularly the New England States, pay for the support of a large number of beneficiaries.

PERKINS INSTITUTION FOR THE BLIND.

The Boston and Albany Railroad Company has earned the gratitude of the business men of Boston by many enterprises, which have both increased its great revenues and added to the commerce of Boston, but by nothing more than by its purchase and extensive use of the Grand Junction Railroad and the Wharf at East Boston. The railroad forms a connection between the main line of the Boston and Albany, and the Fitchburg, Lowell, Eastern, and Boston and Maine Railroads, and gives the Albany road a deep-water connection. Wheat-trains from the West are here emptied of their contents by machinery directly into an elevator, from which in turn vessels may be rapidly loaded. Ample facilities are afforded for loading and unloading the Cunard steamers which swell so largely the tables of exports and imports of this port. And the facilities for the reception and despatch of immigrants at the Grand Junction Wharf are unequalled by those of any other city on the continent. Such as are to continue their journey by land into other States are provided with every comfort, and completely secluded from the sharpers who are always on the look-out for an opportunity to swindle the poor foreigners unused to the customs and often ignorant of the language of the country, until they are sent away in trains over the Grand Junction and the Boston and Albany roads without being compelled even to pass through the city. The amount of business transacted at this wharf is immense. During the six months ending with March, 1872, there were 14,558 cars of freight, with 139,187 tons of merchandise received; and 11,127 cars, loaded with 114,128 tons of freight, were forwarded. In the same time upwards of a million bushels of grain were received at the elevator, and 617,826 bushels were shipped from it for exportation to foreign countries. The railroad and wharves were built in

GRAND JUNCTION WHARVES, EAST BOSTON.

1850-51, and on the occasion of their opening a three days' jubilee was held in Boston, in which many notables, the President of the United States among them, participated. But the sanguine expectations of the people of Boston were not realized until long afterwards. The enterprise did not pay. And when the present owners came into possession of the property in 1868, no train had been run over the road in fourteen years. Vast improvements have been made since then. The manner of doing business at the wharf, as well as its immense amount, is interesting enough to repay amply the trouble of a visit. Our sketch shows the extent of the improvements, and gives a good view of the city from East Boston.

Eliot Square, into which Dudley, Washington, and other streets converge, is a small park in Roxbury, which possesses several points of interest. Here stands the old Unitarian meeting-house of the first church in Roxbury, taking rank in age next after the first church in Boston. Over this church the Rev. Dr. George Putnam has been settled for more than forty years. The dwelling-houses in this square are many of them old, this part of Roxbury having been settled long before the over-crowded streets of Boston sent thousands of the citizens to seek sites for modern villas on the more picturesque hillsides of this and other suburban towns. On this square, too, stands the Norfolk House, a fine building externally, and a favorite boarding-hotel.

FIRST CHURCH IN ROXBURY, AND THE NORFOLK HOUSE.

One of the most important improvements in the Cochituate water-works was made in 1869, when the stand-pipe in Roxbury was erected and put in use. By this simple expedient, which has been found to work admirably in practice, the "head" of water has been increased over the whole city so greatly that the pure water is forced to the highest levels occupied by dwelling-houses. The stand-pipe is on the "Old Fort" lot in Roxbury, between Beech-Glen Avenue and Fort Avenue. The base of the shaft is 158 feet above tide marsh level. The interior pipe is a cylinder of boiler iron, eighty feet long; and around this pipe, but within the exterior wall of brick, is a winding staircase leading to a lookout at the top. The total cost of the structure and the pumping-works connected with it was about $100,000. It was at first intended to supply high service to only those parts of the city at the higher levels, but its capacity was found adequate to the supply of the whole city, and the use of the old reservoir on Beacon Hill was therefore abandoned, though it would doubtless become useful in case of an accident to these works.

Roxbury always had a good reputation for remembering its great men. American cities do not nowadays follow the custom of naming districts or wards after their famous men, and in some of them even the streets are mostly called by numbers. Paris goes to one extreme, commemorating days and historical events by such names as Rue Dix Decembre, Rue de la Dette, changed from Boulevard Haussmann, and so on. New York and Washington go to the other extreme with their Avenue A's, and their Four-and-a-half Streets. Boston has gone but slightly into this unromantic nomenclature, and Roxbury not at all. We have still our Dudley, Eustis, and Warren Streets, and numerous others named in memory of distinguished citizens. General Joseph Warren has been especially remembered, for besides the street which bears his name, there is a steam fire-engine called after him, and the dwelling-house that stands on the spot where his house stood, bears a tablet commemorating the fact. The house stands in a charming site behind a row of fine old trees.

STAND-PIPE OF COCHITUATE WATER-WORKS.

In another part of Roxbury is the famous chromo-lithographic establishment of Prang & Co. The process of making chromos is one of the most interesting of the arts. The care with which each stone must be prepared, every one adding one color, and only one, to the picture that is by and by to appear ; the successive steps by which apparently shapeless patches of color are transformed into excellent and artistic imitations of well-known oil paintings, —these and other facts to be learned by a visit to such an establishment are of great interest. This factory of

WARREN HOUSE.

Prang's is the most extensive of the kind in the country, and it is to the credit of Boston that the reputation of the chromos produced here is not inferior to that of any others. Many, indeed, prefer American lithographs to those made in Europe, and when American chromos are mentioned, it is usually Prang's that are meant.

Dorchester was a delightful old town and a charming new town. It retains its ancient characteristics, and some of the very old houses are still preserved. But its picturesque hills and its fine old woods have within the past few years made it a favorite place for the erection of elegant country residences. On many of the estates vast sums of money were lavished. The skill of the architect and the art of the landscape-gardener were invoked to render these retreats as magnificent as possible. By such means the scenery of Dorchester has been made exceedingly rich and varied. Here the road passes through the midst of large and finely kept estates, surrounding handsome dwelling-

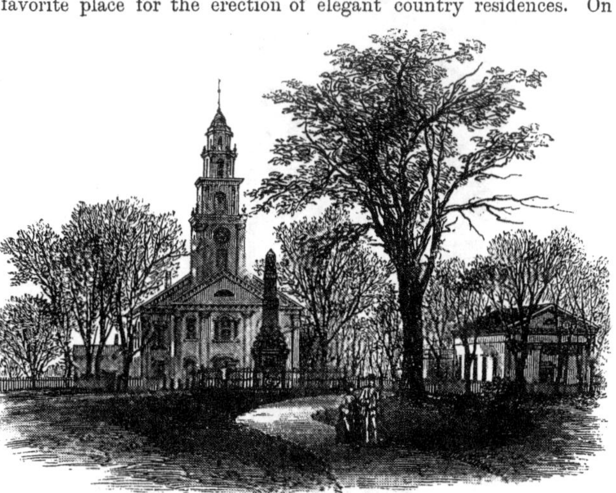

MEETING-HOUSE HILL.

houses, to plunge into a wilderness, where the fields are barren and rocky, and the forests in all their primitive wildness. Again we come upon a thriving village, and pass out of it to find new beauties by the sea-side. We give two views of Dorchester scenery, the one showing Meeting-House Hill, which is one of the landmarks in Dorchester, and the other Savin Hill, as seen from Dorchester Point, — the first belonging to the older part of Dorchester, the latter comparatively new as a place of residence.

SAVIN HILL, FROM OLD COLONY RAILROAD.

The estate known as Grove Hall, at the junction of Warren Street and Blue Hill Avenue, in Dorchester, was purchased for the Consumptives' Home a year or two since, and is now occupied by that and its attendant institutions. It is a very large and spacious mansion, and is surrounded with ample grounds, making the situation a most pleasant retreat for the poor, diseased people who come here for treatment and cure, or for a comfortable home until they are released from suffering by death. The system on which the Consumptives' Home is supported is the same as that upon which the famous orphan asylum of Müller is maintained. The founder was Dr. Charles Cullis, whose attention was drawn, in 1862, to the lack of provision in any existing hospital for persons sick with consumption, and incurable. He began without any funds, and makes it a practice to depend upon daily contributions for the daily wants of the Home. Dr. Cullis calls this institution "A Work of Faith," because he has never solicited any donations, but has prayed to God for aid in the work; and he looks upon the contributions he receives as direct answers to his prayers. The receipts from casual donations, from the proceeds of a fair, and from the estate of the late Miss Nabby Joy, last year, exceeded the sum of fifty-five thousand dollars. During the year there were one hundred and eighty-five patients cared for at the Home, the usual number being from thirty to fifty. Since the opening of the hospital there have been seven hundred and fifty-seven received, of whom only thirty-three were remaining at the close of the year last reported. The plan of the institution is to admit all poor persons sick with consumption, and without home or friends to relieve them, old or young, black or white, native or foreign. All are, in the language of the Report, "freely received in the name of the Lord."

CONSUMPTIVES' HOME, DORCHESTER.

Boston harbor is protected by the natural breakwater on which stands the town of Hull. This is a very singular peninsula, jutting northward from the South Shore, and partially enclosing a very extensive tract of water. Hull has several points of interest. Nantasket Beach, on the side of the peninsula towards the sea, is one of the finest on the coast, and it has therefore become a favorite place of resort in the summer for thousands of the citizens of Boston. The summer population is largest at the lower or southern end of the peninsula, while the permanent population is mostly concentrated near the other extremity. It is the latter part of the town that is represented by our view. On the high hill, which overlooks the entire entrance to Boston Harbor, is situated the observatory, from which the arrival of vessels, their names, and the point whence they come are telegraphed immediately to the Merchants' Exchange in the city. Hull is one of the smallest towns in Massachusetts, and there have been many jokes at its expense on this account. The vote of the town is almost always one of the first returned at a general election. From this there has arisen the curious saying, "As goes Hull, so goes the State," — a saying which is very far from true. Dr. Holmes said in his Autocrat of the Breakfast-Table, that in this town they read a famous line with a mispronunciation pardonable under the circumstances, —

"All are but parts of one stupendous Hull."

The harbor of Boston is filled with islands, most of which have a history that it would be exceedingly interesting to recount. In the summer season there are numerous steamboats plying between the city and the many places of resort in the harbor and just outside of it. For almost the smallest of fees one may steam in and out

VIEW OF HULL.

between the several islands, and enjoy, on the most sultry of days, a cool and refreshing breeze, together with the most delightful and ever-changing scenery. Among a great many points of interest only a very few can be here mentioned, and we confine ourselves to the lighthouses and some of the fortifications. The first fort built upon Castle Island was constructed in 1634, and since that time the island has always been fortified. The works have been rebuilt a great many times. Castle William stood on this island when the Revolutionary war broke out, and when the British troops were obliged to evacuate Boston they destroyed the fort and burned it to ashes. The Provincial forces then took possession of the island, and restored the fort. In 1798 its name was formally changed to Fort Independence, — the President, John Adams, being present on the occasion. In 1798 the island was ceded to the United States. From 1785 until 1805 this fort was the place appointed for the confinement of prisoners sentenced to hard labor, provision having been made in the act of cession to the United States that this privilege should be retained. The present fort is of quite recent construction.

Directly opposite Fort Independence, as one enters or leaves the inner harbor by the main ship-channel, is the still uncompleted fortification named Fort Winthrop, on Governor's Island. The island was granted to Governor Winthrop in 1632, and was subsequently confirmed to his heirs. In 1640, the conditions of his ownership having already been once previously changed, he was granted the island on condition of paying one bushel of apples to the Governor and one to the General Court in winter, annually. It continued in the sole possession of the Winthrop family until 1808, when a part of it was sold to the government

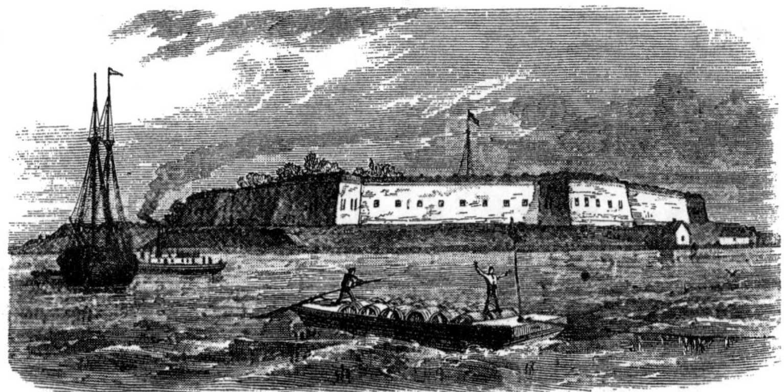

FORT INDEPENDENCE.

for the purpose of erecting a fort, which was named Fort Warren. The name given to the work now in process of erection is Fort Winthrop, in honor of the Governor of Massachusetts Bay and first owner of the island, while the name of the former fort has been transferred to the fortification further down the harbor. When fully completed, Fort Winthrop is intended to be a most important defence to the harbor.

FORT WINTHROP.

Fort Warren is situated on George's Island, near the entrance to the harbor, and is the most famous of all the defences of the city. George's Island was claimed as the property of James Pemberton of Hull as early as 1622. His possession of it having been confirmed, it was bought, sold, and inherited by numerous owners, until 1825, when it became the property of the city of Boston. It is now, of course, under the jurisdiction of the United States government. The construction of the present fort was begun in April, 1833, and was completed in 1850. The material is finely hammered Quincy granite, and the stone faces, as well as those parts that have been protected with earth and sodded over, are as neat and trim as art can make them. The fort is one of great strength, but it has never yet been needed to defend the harbor of Boston. During the Rebellion, it was used as a place of confinement for noted Confederate prisoners, the most famous of all being the rebel commissioners to Europe, Mason and Slidell, who were sent here for confinement after their capture on board the Trent by Commodore Wilkes.

FORT WARREN, BOSTON HARBOR.

About two miles from Fort Warren, nearly due east, and at the entrance of the harbor, is the Boston Light. The island on which it stands has been used as a lighthouse station since 1715, when the General Court of the colony passed the necessary acts. The land was generously given to the colony by the owners of it, though as there is soil on only about three quarters of an acre, the rest of the two or three acres being bare, jagged rock, the gift entailed no great loss upon them. In the time of the Revolution, the lighthouse was the object of much small warfare, and was several times destroyed and rebuilt. In 1783 it was once more restored by the State, being built this time of stone; and it is this lighthouse which still stands at the mouth of the harbor, though it has since been enlarged and refitted several times. The top of the lighthouse now stands ninety-eight feet above the level of the sea, and is fitted with a revolving light which can be seen from a distance of sixteen nautical miles in fair weather.

BOSTON LIGHT.

Still nearer to Fort Warren, and on the direct line to Boston Light, is the Spit, or Bug Light. It is a curious structure. The lower part is a system of iron pillars fixed in the rock, affording no surface for the waves to beat against and destroy. The fixed red light is about thirty-five feet above the level of the sea, and can be seen at a distance of about seven miles in clear weather. This light was built in 1856. Its object is to warn navigators of the dangerous obstacle known as Harding's Ledge, about two miles out at sea, east of Point Allerton, at the head of Nantasket Beach.

BUG LIGHT.

The lighthouse on Long Island was built in 1819. The tower is twenty-two feet in height, but the light is eighty feet above the level of the sea. The tower is of iron painted white ; the lantern has nine burners ; the light is fixed, and can be seen in a clear night about fifteen miles. The object of the light is to assist in the navigation of the harbor. The government is at present erecting on Long Island head a strong battery, which has not yet been named. There have been several attempts to make Long Island a place for summer residences. There has been a hotel on the island for some years, but it has been popular only intermittently. There is no good reason why these charming islands should not be so occupied in preference to some of the more distant points on the coast, where only occasional

LONG ISLAND LIGHT.

cool breezes relieve the heat of summer. An admirable suggestion has been made, that the city purchase Long Island, or some other large island in the harbor, and convert it into a park, to which visitors might be carried on the payment of a fare no larger than is demanded for a ride in the horse-cars.

East of Long Island head there is a low, rocky island on which stands a singularly shaped monument. It consists of a solid structure of stone, twelve feet in height, and forty feet square. All the stones in this piece of masonry are securely fastened together with copper. Upon it stands an octagonal pyramid of wood, twenty feet high, and painted black. It is supposed that this monument was erected in the earliest years of the present century, though the date is not known. Its purpose was to warn vessels of one of the most dangerous shoals in the harbor. This island is known as Nix's Mate, though for what reason is not known. There is a tradition, unsupported by facts, that the mate of a vessel of which one Captain Nix was master, was executed upon the island for killing the latter. But it was known as "Nixes Iland," as long ago as 1636, and this would seem to dispose of the story. It is, however, true, that several murderers and pirates have been hanged upon the island, and one William Fly was hanged there in chains in 1726 for the crime of piracy, on which occasion, the Boston News Letter informs us, Fly "behaved himself very unbecomingly, even to the last." It is a part of the tradition above referred to that Nix's mate declared his innocence, and asserted, as a proof of it, that the island would be washed away. If any such prophecy was ever made, it has certainly been fulfilled. We know by the records that it contained in the neighborhood of twelve acres in 1636;

NIX'S MATE.

there is now not more than one acre of shoal, and there is not a vestige of soil remaining.

Point Shirley is the southern extremity of the town of Winthrop, but it properly comes into any notice of Boston harbor. Its chief attraction is Taft's Hotel, noted for its game dinners. Indeed Point Shirley, ever since it received its present name, has been synonymous with good cheer. A company of merchants purchased it in

POINT SHIRLEY.

1753, designing to establish a fishery station. They never put the property to its intended use, but when they were ready to advertise the place, they invited Governor Shirley to go down to the spot with them. He accepted, the party had a fine time and a fine dinner, and, by permission of his Excellency, what had before been known as Pulling Point was dubbed Point Shirley. The name of Pulling Point has since been transferred to another point of land on the same peninsula.

We have only glanced at the harbor and a few of the numerous places of interest in and about it. The merest mention only can be made of some of the other points that are worthy of being seen, and of being illustrated and described. The islands in the harbor are many, and of very peculiar shapes, which fact has given some of them their names, — as, for instance, Spectacle, Half Moon, and Apple Islands. Few of them are occupied, and many are uninhabitable, but the sail among and around them is in the summer time a most agreeable change from the hot brick walls and dusty streets of the city. If we extend our view beyond the harbor along the north shore we shall see Revere Beach, — one of the finest on the coast, — Lynn, and Nahant. Both the latter places may easily be visited by steamers. Nahant is perhaps the chief glory of the north shore. It is a peninsula connected with the mainland at Lynn by a long narrow neck, upon which is a noble beach. Those who dwell upon the peninsula regard its comparative inaccessibility as something strongly in its favor. They have not allowed a hotel to be erected upon it since the destruction by fire of one that formerly stood in the town. Nahant is a favorite resort for picnickers, for whom a place has been specially provided which is fantastically called Maolis Gardens, — Maolis being nothing more than Siloam spelled backwards. For the rest, Nahant is occupied by wealthy citizens of Boston who have erected for themselves in this secluded place elegant summer residences where, in the midst of their gardens and groves and lawns, they may live as freely and as quietly as they wish. The sea-view is magnificent. The peninsula lies near to the entrance of Boston harbor, and is practically an island at some distance from the coast. All the grandeur of the sea in a storm, and all the beauty of the sea on a fine day when the horizon is dotted with the white sails of arriving and departing vessels, the dwellers at Nahant enjoy at their grandest and most beautiful. Beyond Nahant are Egg Rock, a small island still farther than Nahant from the coast; Marblehead Neck and Point, which are rapidly coming into favor as summer resorts; Swampscott, already one of the most fashionable of the coast watering-places; and Cape Ann, with its succession of beautiful sea-side villages, — Beverly Farms, Manchester, Gloucester, Rockport, and Pigeon Cove. On the south coast we may find equally interesting and equally beautiful places. At Hingham, among other objects to be noticed, is the oldest church edifice in the country; and off Cohasset is the famous Minot's Ledge Lighthouse, a solid stone structure that stands where a former lighthouse was destroyed by a storm some years ago, on one of the most dangerous and most dreaded rocks upon our coast.

VII. THE SUBURBS.

NO other city in the country can boast such suburbs as Boston has. For extent and beauty, they are unrivalled. The picturesque hills, separated by beautifully winding rivers, make, of themselves, an ever-varied picture of charming landscape. Art has added greatly to the beauties which nature has so lavishly scattered. Almost every available site for a fine country residence has been occupied, and all that wealth could do to improve upon natural attractions has been done. But this is not all. Large cities and a score of flourishing towns have sprung up, where city and country are pleasantly commingled ; and everywhere throughout the large district of which Boston is the centre may be seen the evidences of industry and thrift, excellent roads, neat fences and hedges, thriving gardens and orchards, comfortable, tastefully built, and well-painted houses. Nor are these towns and cities destitute of a history, which, did space permit, should be told at length. We can merely glance at a few of the more noticeable objects of interest in some of these surrounding places, leaving it to each citizen and visitor to search out the others, with the assurance that one can hardly go astray in seeking for them, whatever be the direction taken.

BUNKER HILL MONUMENT.

The first object to be noticed is the grand monument erected in Charlestown to commemorate the battle of Bunker Hill ; but the monument needs no description. The event it celebrates and the consequences of that event, the appearance of this imposing granite shaft, and the magnificent view of the entire surrounding country to be obtained from its observatory, are, or should be, familiar to every citizen of New England ; and no visitor to Boston from more distant parts of the country is likely to return home without ascending the monument as a good patriot. The oration delivered by Daniel Webster at the dedication of the monument on the anniversary of the battle of Bunker Hill, the 17th of June, 1843, has been declaimed by every school-boy. That anniversary is still, and should long remain, a holiday, — a day to be celebrated in Charlestown and throughout the State and country as long as the Republic, which owes so much to that memorable contest, shall stand.

THE NAVY YARD, FROM EAST BOSTON.

No visitor to Charlestown should leave it until he has visited the United States Navy Yard, established by the government in the year 1800. The yard has since been very greatly enlarged, and extensive and costly buildings have been erected upon it. The dry dock, which was begun in July, 1827, and completed six years later, is a magnificent and most substantial work of granite masonry, 341 feet long, 80 feet wide, and 30 feet deep, which cost even in those days of low prices $675,000. The granite ropewalk too, the finest structure of the kind in the country, and a quarter of a mile in length, will not fail to attract attention. Several of the largest vessels of our old navy were built at this yard. Of late, while the government has been reducing, rather than increasing, its naval force, the work here has been confined chiefly to repairs upon old vessels, and the busy activity of past years is no longer seen.

The United States Marine Hospital at Chelsea, which appears on the right in the background of our sketch, is a large and handsome structure upon the crest of a high hill, near the mouth of the Mystic River. This institution, as well as the Naval Hospital, at the foot of the same hill, was erected and is maintained by the general government for the benefit of invalid sailors. The situation is salubrious, and the prospect from the Marine Hospital, overlooking as it does the harbor and two or three cities, is very fine.

Passing now into Cambridge, we must first notice it as the site of the most famous, as well as most ancient, university in the country. It was but six years after the settlement of Boston that the General Court appropriated four hundred pounds for the establishment of a school or college at Newtown, as Cambridge was then called. As this sum was equal to a whole year's tax of the entire colony, we may infer in what estimation the earliest colonists held a liberal education. Two years after, the institution received the liberal bequest of eight hundred pounds from the estate of the Rev. John Harvard, an English clergyman, who died at Charlestown in 1638. The General Court, in consequence of this bequest, named the college after its generous benefactor, and changed the name of the town where it was located to Cambridge, Mr. Harvard having been educated at Cambridge in

GORE HALL, HARVARD COLLEGE.

old England. The college was thus placed on a firm foundation, and by good management and the prevalence of liberal ideas, under the fostering care of the Colony and the State, and the almost lavish generosity of alumni and other friends, it has assumed and steadily maintained the leading position among the colleges of the country, its only rival being Yale. The college long ago became a university. Schools of law, medicine, dentistry, theology, science, mining, and agriculture, have been established in connection with it, each endowed with its own funds, and each independent of all the others, except that all are under one general management. The college yard contains a little more than twenty-two acres, and nearly the whole available space is already occupied by the numerous buildings required by an institution of such magnitude. An important change has been made within the past few years in the government of the university; the overseers, constituting the second

VIEW OF HARVARD COLLEGE: THE QUADRANGLE.

and more numerous branch of the university legislature, were originally the Governor and Deputy-Governor, with all the magistrates, and the ministers of the six adjoining towns. After numerous changes, which were, however, only changes in the manner of selecting the clergymen who should constitute this board, the power of choosing the overseers was, in 1851, vested in the Legislature. All this system has since been abolished. The graduates of the college have been granted the privilege of choosing the entire board; and every member of it, as now constituted, has been elected by this constituency. The advantages of thus making those who are most interested in the good management of the college partially responsible for its government were at once apparent, and other colleges have not been slow in practising upon so satisfactory an experiment. Another change, which has been gradually going on for some years, gives students a much wider range of studies than formerly. The number of elective studies has very greatly increased, and one is not now, as formerly, compelled to pursue a fixed and unalterable course, but may choose the branches he will pursue in accordance with his tastes and his intended business in life. The number of students in all branches of the university, by the latest catalogue, was 1214. There are nine libraries connected with the university, containing in all about 192,000 volumes, of which 128,000 are in the college library in Gore Hall, a view of which we give. The university is now under the able presidency of Charles W. Eliot.

Cambridge is noted not only for being the seat of the first college in America, but for having been the first place in the country where a printing-press was set up. In 1639 a press was brought over from England, and put in operation in the house of the President, who had the sole charge of it for many years. The first thing printed upon it was the Freeman's Oath, followed by an Almanack for New England, and the Psalms "newly turned into meter." A fragment of the last-named work is preserved in the college library, and copies of it may still be seen in some antiquarian libraries. Cambridge has at the present day some of the largest and most completely furnished printing-offices in America, conspicuous among which is the University Press of Welch, Bigelow, & Co.

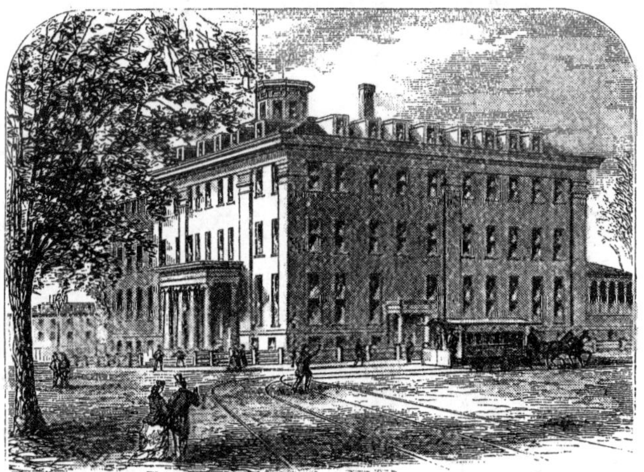

THE UNIVERSITY PRESS, CAMBRIDGE.

Their office is one of the most celebrated in the country for the quality and accuracy of its work. Many of the hundreds of thousands of books published annually in Boston, and not a few of those issued by publishers in New York, including illustrated books requiring the finest workmanship and the greatest care, are printed and bound at this establishment.

Not very far from the college grounds stands one of the few famous trees of the country, — the Washington Elm, — the only survivor of the ancient forest that originally covered all this part of Cambridge. It was under this tree that General Washington took command of the Continental army on the morning of the 3d of July, 1775.* A neat fence surrounds this giant of the ancient forest, and an inscription commemorates the important event which was the most interesting in its centuries of existence.

THE WASHINGTON ELM, CAMBRIDGE.

At a short distance from this famous elm, on the road to Watertown, near Brattle Street, stands the house used by the patriot general as his headquarters. It was previously the residence of Colonel John Vassal, a royalist or Tory, but was used by General Washington on its abandonment by the owner; and here continued to be

RESIDENCE OF H. W. LONGFELLOW.

the head-quarters of the American army, for the greater part of the time, until the evacuation of Boston by the British in the spring of 1776. The house stands in a large and beautiful lot of ground, a little distance from the street, in the midst of tall trees and shrubbery, and though in a style of architecture different from that now generally employed, it is still an elegant residence in external appearance, while the rich and costly finish of the interior has been preserved by its successive owners. The present possessor and occupant of this noble estate is the poet, Henry Wadsworth Longfellow, and surely there is more than poetic fitness in such an occupation of a house around which cling so many historical associations.

ENTRANCE TO MOUNT AUBURN.

Mount Auburn Cemetery is situated partly in Cambridge and partly in Watertown. The land was originally purchased and improved by the Massachusetts Horticultural Society for an experimental garden. It subsequently passed into the hands of the trustees of Mount Auburn Cemetery, and was consecrated in the year 1831. It is now one of the most extensive cities of the dead used by the people of Boston, being in extent about one hundred and twenty-five acres. The surface is remarkably diversified, giving unusual opportunities to the landscape - gardener to improve the nat-

CHAPEL, MOUNT AUBURN.

ural beauty of the scenery. There are several sheets of water, and high hills and deep vales in abundance. Trees in great variety have been transplanted into this enclosure, adding greatly to its beauty. Upon the summit of the highest hill, Mount Auburn proper, a stone tower has been erected, from which a very fine view of all the surrounding country can be obtained. Many elegant and costly monuments adorn the grounds in every part. Some of these have been erected and the expense defrayed by public subscription, but many more by the surviving friends of the thousands who here sleep the last sleep. The granite entrance-gate was designed from an Egyptian model, and was erected at a cost of about ten thousand dollars. The very beautiful chapel was built in 1848, at an expense of twenty-five thousand dollars. It is used for funeral services at the cemetery. There are around the walls, within, several excellent statues and memorials, one of which, a statue of James Otis, by Crawford, is particularly to be admired.

The history of the Boston Waterworks is exceedingly interesting. The original introduction of water is described on page 28. The growth of the city has been so wonderful that what was originally calculated to be a sufficient supply of water for half a century was, in a few years, found to be inadequate. Again and again have measures been taken to make good the deficiency, but it is only within the present year (1872) that a comprehensive scheme has been entered upon, which, when completed, will, it is believed, avert for an indefinite period all fears of a water famine. One of the works which formed a part of the original system is the Brookline Reservoir. This was a natural basin, protected on all sides except on the north. A puddled embankment was constructed on this side, and the interior of the entire basin protected from washing by a sloping wall, and the reservoir proper was complete. The reservoir marks the terminus of the brick conduit leading from Lake Cochituate. From the reservoir to the city the water is conducted by iron mains. There are two gate-houses, one at either end of the reservoir. The whole surface of water, when the reservoir is full, covers about twenty-three acres, and its capacity to a point two feet below the top of the dam is nearly one hundred and twenty million gallons.

ENTRANCE TO THE RESERVOIR GROUNDS.

The necessity for building a new reservoir, for the purpose of storing the water that usually ran to waste over the dam at Lake Cochituate during and after the spring

THE DRIVE, SHOWING THE LARGE RESERVOIR.

GATE HOUSE, CHESTNUT HILL.

and fall freshets, was urged by the Water Board in 1863, but nothing was then done about it. The next year the City Council began to move in the matter. In 1865 the Legislature gave the necessary authority to the city. Purchases of land were immediately made, and the work begun. More than two hundred acres of land, costing about $120,000, were deeded to the city before the reservoir was finished. Like the Brookline Reservoir, it constituted a natural basin. It is five miles from the Boston City Hall, and one mile from the Brookline Reservoir. It lies in the towns of Newton and Brookline, near Chestnut Hill, from which it derives its name. It is, in fact, a double reservoir, being divided by a water-tight dam into two basins of irregular shape. The surface of water in both is about one hundred and twenty-five acres, and when filled to their fullest capacity the two basins will hold nearly eight hundred million gallons, or a sufficient supply for the entire city for several weeks. As we have said, even

THE DRIVE, ON THE MARGIN OF THE SMALL RESERVOIR.

this addition to the works has been found inadequate, and during the present year (1872) authority has been given to the city to take water from the Sudbury River. It is intended to procure a temporary supply by connecting the river with Lake Cochituate, and subsequently to bring the water to the reservoirs by independent mains.

JAMAICA POND, NORTH VIEW.

The Chestnut Hill Reservoir is not only a great benefit to the city in its practical uses, it is also a great pleasure resort. A magnificent driveway, varying from sixty to eighty feet in width, surrounds the entire work, and is one of the greatest attractions of the suburbs of Boston. It is, in fact, the most popular drive in the vicinity. In some parts the road runs along close to the embankment, separated from it only by the beautiful gravelled walk with the sodding on either side. Elesewhere it leaves the embankment and rises to a higher level at a little distance, from which an uninterrupted view of the entire reservoir can be had. The scenery in the neighborhood is so varied that it would of itself make this region a delightful one for pleasure driving, without the added attractions of the charming sheet of water, the graceful curvatures of the road, and the neat, trim appearance of the greensward that lines it throughout its entire length.

Before the introduction of water from Lake Cochituate the city was dependent upon wells and springs, and upon Jamaica Pond, in the town of West Roxbury. A company was incorporated in 1795 to bring water into Boston from that source, and its powers were enlarged by subsequent acts. It was for a long time a bad investment for the shareholders. Afterwards the company had a greater degree of prosperity, and at one time it supplied at least fifteen hundred houses in Boston. The water was conveyed through the streets by four main pipes, consisting of pine logs. Two of these were of four inches, and two of three inches bore. The water thus brought into the city was conveyed nearly as far north as State Street. In 1840 an iron main, ten inches in diameter, was laid through the whole length of Tremont Street to Bowdoin Square. The company was ready to increase the supply very largely, but the prospective wants of the city were far beyond the capacity of Jamaica Pond to supply, and the Lake Cochituate enterprise not only prevented the aqueduct company from enlarging its operations, but rendered all its outlay in Boston useless and valueless. The city, however, made compensation by purchasing the franchise and property for the sum of $45,000, in 1851. The property, minus the franchise, which the city of course wished to extinguish, was sold in 1856 for $32,000. At this time the pipes were disconnected at the Roxbury line, but those in Boston were never taken up. At present the chief practical use of Jamaica Pond is to furnish in winter a great quantity of ice, which is cut and stored in the large houses on its banks for consumption in the warm weather. It is a great resort for young and some older people in the winter for skating. Beautiful residences line its banks, and the drive around it is one of the most beautiful of the many which make the suburbs of Boston so attractive to its own citizens and to strangers. In summer there is much pleasure sailing and rowing on the pond, and in past years there have been several interesting regattas upon it.

JAMAICA POND, SOUTH SIDE.

Forest Hills Cemetery, also in the

town of West Roxbury, was originally established by the city of Roxbury, of which the town at the time formed a part. It was subsequently conveyed to the predecessors of the present proprietors. It is a little larger in territory than Mount Auburn, but it is by no means so crowded as the older cemetery. It contains a great number of interesting memorials of persons, some of them eminent in the history of State and nation, who have gone. The burial-lot of the Warren family is on the summit of Mount Warren. The remains of General Joseph Warren, who fell at Bunker Hill, have been taken from the Old Granary Burying-ground in Boston, and reinterred in this cemetery. Within two or three years the finest receiving-tomb in any cemetery in the country has been built at Forest Hills. The portico is nearly thirty feet square, and is built in the Gothic style of architecture in Concord granite. Its appearance is massive, without being cumbersome. Within there are two hundred and eighty-six catacombs, each for a single coffin, which are closely sealed up after an interment. The entrance gateway to Forest Hills Cemetery is a very elegant, costly, and imposing structure of Roxbury stone and Caledonia freestone. The inscription upon the face of the outer gateway is, —

ENTRANCE TO FOREST HILLS.

"I AM THE RESURRECTION AND THE LIFE,"

in golden letters. On the inner face is in similar letters the inscription, —

"HE THAT KEEPETH THEE WILL NOT SLUMBER."

The grounds of the cemetery, like those of Mount Auburn, are exceedingly picturesque, the variety of hill and dale, greensward, thickets of trees, pleasant sheets of water, and rocky eminences, making the place an exceedingly attractive spot to wander and read the story of lives that are spent. And the hand of art has added much to the natural beauty of the place.

It is by no means to be understood that in our glance at the suburbs we have exhausted the subject. There are a great many other points that should be visited. The magnificent beach in Revere is of itself a sight well worth the time spent in driving thither. A short visit should be made to Lynn, the head-quarters of the shoe manufacture, and another to the extensive factories of Lowell and Lawrence. In the church at Quincy are the tombs of the two Presidents Adams. Brookline, Newton, Belmont, and Arlington are most beautiful towns, and in all the environs are charming drives through the pleasantest of districts. At Watertown is the great United States Arsenal; the battle-grounds of Concord and Lexington are within easy reach by railroad; and, in fact, no route can be taken out of the city that does not lead to some point where the stranger will find much that is both pleasing and interesting.

The original design of this book has now been accomplished. We have mentioned, illustrated, and described the principal objects of interest in Boston and its vicinity; at the same time we have purposely avoided giving a guide-book character to "Boston Illustrated." The intention has been to describe permanent objects of interest only. But in a supplement which accompanies and forms a part of this book will be found all the information necessary for a stranger in Boston. This supplement is not only a guide-book, but a condensed directory of the city, and it contains an account of the World's Peace Jubilee and International Musical Festival of 1872, and a description of the Coliseum in which it is to be held.

INDEX TO TEXT.

ALPHABETICAL INDEX TO BUSINESS ANNOUNCEMENTS.

Below is an index to the Business Announcements made in "Boston Illustrated" by some of the oldest and most reliable houses, including the leading hotels, newspapers, etc.

CONTENTS.

LIST OF ILLUSTRATIONS.

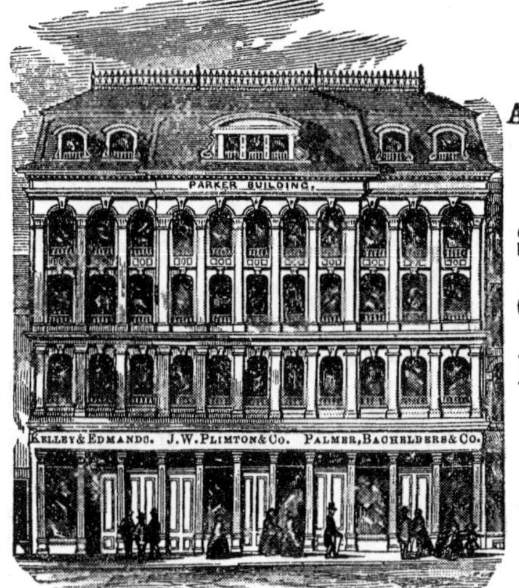

Eſtabliſhed 1817.

AMERICAN AND FOREIGN

WATCHES,

Sterling Silver Ware,

Gorham Plated Goods,

Paris Mantel Clocks,

Parlor Bronzes,

Stone Cameos,

Diamonds.

PALMER, BACHELDERS, & CO.,

162 Washington Street, Boston.

J. W. PLIMPTON & CO.,

IMPORTERS AND JOBBERS OF

RIBBONS, SILKS, MILLINERY,

STRAW GOODS, &c.,

No. 158 Washington Street, ... Boston.

KELLEY & EDMANDS,

IMPORTERS OF

FANCY GOODS

AND

MERCHANDISE FOR DRUGGISTS,

No. 156 Washington Street, Boston.

CALDER & OTIS,

FLORISTS AND FLORAL SEEDSMEN,

Hotel Boylston,

TREMONT, COR. BOYLSTON STREET,

BOSTON.

We take pleasure in informing our friends and the public, that we have leased for a term of years the store corner of Tremont and Boylston Streets, in HOTEL BOYLSTON (a pictorial representation of which may be found in text of this book), for the purpose of transacting business as

FLORISTS AND FLORAL SEEDSMEN,

and dealers in all articles pertaining to the growth and cultivation of Flowers, and are prepared to furnish every description of Floral Work and Design, suitable for WEDDINGS, PARTIES, FUNERALS, etc. ; also, Cut Flowers in quantity, and Plants in pots. We possess peculiar advantages in having, each of us, very extensive Greenhouses, long established, the products of which we have hitherto sold at wholesale to the dealers in Flowers in Boston and New York.

Patrons may rely upon receiving prompt and courteous attention.

CALDER & OTIS.

AUGUSTUS P. CALDER,
Residence and Greenhouses, Blue Hill Avenue,
Boston Highlands.

THEODORE C. OTIS,
Residence, Townsend St., Boston Highlands,
Greenhouses in Wellesley.

GEO. W. CHIPMAN & CO.,

Carpetings, Carpet Lining,

AND

WINDOW SHADES,

AT WHOLESALE AND RETAIL.

Nos. 93 Court and 5 Hanover Streets,

BOSTON.

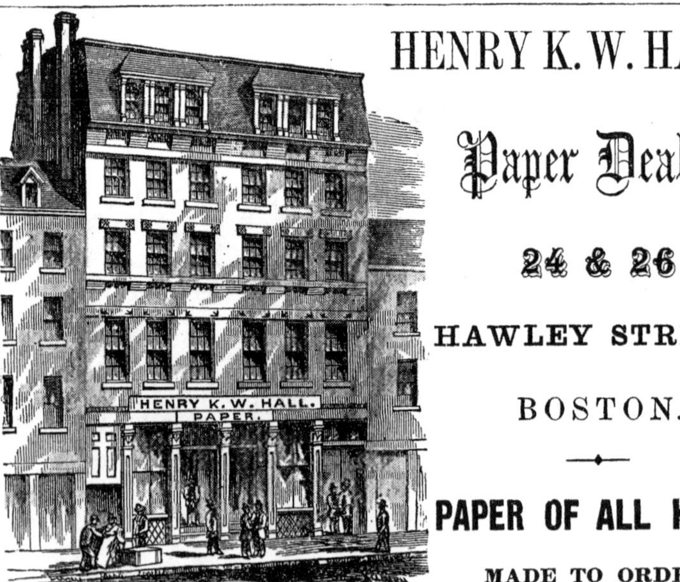

HENRY K. W. HALL,

Paper Dealer,

24 & 26

HAWLEY STREET,

BOSTON.

PAPER OF ALL KINDS

MADE TO ORDER.

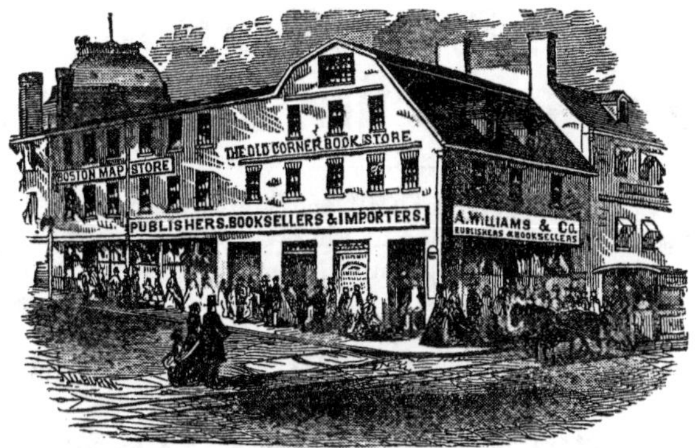

Erected A. D. 1712.

A. WILLIAMS & CO.,

BOOKSELLERS AND PUBLISHERS,

Established 1841,

135 Washington Street, Boston,

KNOWN AS THE

OLD CORNER BOOKSTORE.

A. W. & CO. respectfully invite the attention of gentlemen and ladies visiting the city to their large and varied stock of Books in every department of literature, in elegant as well as plain bindings. The stock is selected with great care, and with special reference to making this famous corner a

FIRST-CLASS RETAIL BOOKSTORE.

Connected therewith will be found specialties, such as

SCIENTIFIC AND PRACTICAL HANDBOOKS FOR THE MECHANIC.
AGRICULTURAL AND HORTICULTURAL BOOKS.
MEDICAL AND SURGICAL BOOKS.

Of the above, probably no place in town offers a larger variety or a more complete assortment. A. W. & CO. have recently added a new department, to which they are constantly making additions by every steamer from Europe, viz.: —

ALL THE NEW ENGLISH BOOKS.

Beautiful London Juvenile Books and

LONDON TOY-BOOKS

in great variety.

A. W. & CO. are one of the original founders of the Periodical Trade in the United States; disposing of the wholesale part thereof, they have retained and added to their store one of the best

PERIODICAL COUNTERS

in the city of Boston; thus aiming to make their store one of the most useful, and (they trust) most agreeable places of resort in the city. Strangers will find a complete assortment of

GUIDE-BOOKS, MAPS, GLOBES,

thus affording to strangers visiting the city a convenient and pleasant place of visiting for amusement and literary resort. Please recollect the store, corner School and Washington Streets, near the City Hall, Parker and Tremont Houses.

A. WILLIAMS & CO.

JAMES CAMPBELL,

Publisher, Bookseller, and Stationer.

Standard Works, in elegant Calf and Morocco bindings.
Illustrated Books, with elegant Engravings by eminent artists.
Bibles and Prayer Books, in the best styles of English bindings.
Juvenile and Toy Books in great profusion, to suit all tastes.

English, French, and American Stationery,

ALL OF WHICH ARE OFFERED

AT THE VERY LOWEST PRICES.

Books Imported to Order, with promptness, at the lowest prices.
Special attention given to **Medical and Scientific Books.**

CATALOGUES, IN U. S. CURRENCY,

SENT FREE ON APPLICATION TO

JAMES CAMPBELL, 18 Tremont Street, Museum Building (a pictorial representation of which may be found in the text of this book), **Boston, Mass.**

H. M. CLARKE & CO.,

MANUFACTURERS AND DEALERS IN

Fine Book and News Paper.

PAPER AND STOCK WAREHOUSE,

89 Milk & 90 Congress Streets,

BOSTON.

Where to find

Where Machinery can be bought, sold, or exchanged, what new Mills, Manufacturing Enterprises, &c., are being started. The Manufacturing News of the United States.

Where to find

The Gossip of Trade, Movements, Prices, and news of all descriptions of Merchandise, and operations of buyers and sellers.

Where to find

The only weekly list of the Business Changes in the United States, New Firms, Dissolutions, Withdrawals, &c.

Where to find

Money Matters, Mining, Railroad and Insurance Intelligence, presented in a terse and readable style, spiced with Original Articles on all live topics by the best writers, Wit, Humor, Literary Notes, Sketches by Talented Authors, Dramatic Criticisms, &c.

IN THE

Boston Commercial Bulletin.

TERMS, . . . $4.00 A YEAR.

☞ **SAMPLES SENT FREE.**

Address CURTIS GUILD & CO.,
Boston, Mass

CHOICE! CHARMING!! CHEAP!!!

The Nursery:

A MONTHLY MAGAZINE FOR YOUNGEST READERS.

This unique and much admired work, begun in 1867, retains its

Unrivalled Corps of Contributors and Artists,

and gives **in every number** a profusion of the

CHOICEST PICTURES,

executed in the **best and most costly style,** and designed especially for the young.

☞ **Subscriptions may begin with any Number.**

TERMS:

$1.50 a Year, in advance; . . 15 cents a Single Number.

PUBLISHED BY JOHN L. SHOREY,
36 Bromfield Street, Boston, Mass.

BOSTON THEATRE.

MR. J. B. BOOTH, . . . Lessee and Manager.

This is the most beautiful, as well as the largest, Theatre in America. The edifice stands on a lot extending from Washington to Mason Street, the main entrance being from 353 – 363 Washington Street. The unpretending appearance of the exterior is more than atoned for in the richness of decoration and grandeur of proportion which a view of the interior presents. The auditorium is circular in form, and the seats are so arranged that each one commands a full view of the stage. The Theatre is lighted by a massive chandelier suspended from the dome, which has five hundred and twelve burners and two hundred thousand glittering prisms. The stage is very capacious and complete, and amply provided with every species of mechanism which may be wanted for the production of effects.

The acoustics of the building are perfect, and four thousand persons can hear distinctly the faintest word or note spoken or sung on the stage. The seating capacity of the house is for three thousand four hundred persons, and fully one thousand more have eligible standing room.

The best dramatic and operatic performances alternate throughout the season, and all artists of distinction make their appearance here, so that patrons always enjoy the best class of entertainments. Visitors and strangers to the "Hub," desirous of viewing the several "institutions" which have made it so renowned, should not neglect to visit the

BOSTON THEATRE.

Performances are given every evening of the week and on Saturday afternoons. The current attractions are noted in the daily newspapers and bills of the day.

MR. J. M. WARD, Treasurer.

MR. H. A. M'GLENEN, Business Agent.

EING proprietors of the first press established in the country, — widely known as the UNIVERSITY PRESS, — and having every resource of typography at our command, our large experience in Book-making and superior facilities for

ELECTROTYPING, PRINTING, AND BINDING

enable us to execute with ACCURACY and DESPATCH every description of FINE PRINTING; and we would call the attention of authors and publishers to such books of our manufacture as Gesenius's Hebrew Grammar, Harris's Insects of Massachusetts, Baird's Birds of California, Whittier's Snow-Bound, The American Enterprise, Beecher's Life of Christ, Crosby's and Goodwin's Greek Grammars and Readers, Whitney's Yosemite Guide-Book, Woodbury's German Grammar, Leighton's Latin Lessons, and numerous other classic, miscellaneous, and scientific works bearing our imprint, as specimens of the beauty and correctness of our printing.

We have an *extensive* and *carefully selected* assortment of

MODERN AND OLD STYLE TYPE

from the best foundries in Europe and America, a large variety of ORNAMENTAL INITIAL LETTERS of new and original designs, with HEAD and TAIL PIECES to match, and everything in the line of typography to give the page an attractive appearance.

We have also the most improved

Printing Machinery

in the country, including the *largest Adams Presses*, *Hoe's Stop Cylinders* and *largest Drum Cylinders*, and the only *Plating Machine* in any printing-office in America, — invaluable in fine CUT PRINTING, of which we make a specialty.

Employing expert proof-readers and the most skilful workmen, and giving our *personal attention* to every detail of our extensive business, we feel confident we shall continue to maintain our reputation for

ACCURATE AND ELEGANT PRINTING

in all its various branches.

WELCH, BIGELOW, & CO.

Mercantile Savings Institution,

No. 387 WASHINGTON STREET,

BOSTON.

(See design of Building in text of this book.)

SIX PER CENT INTEREST PAID ON DEPOSITS remaining in Bank from April 1st to October 1st, or from October 1st to April 1st; all other deposits will draw interest at the rate of five per cent for every full calendar month they remain in bank. This is the only Savings-Bank in the State that pays interest on deposits for every full month, and the only Savings Institution that has a paid-up guarantee fund (of $205,000.00) **for the express protection of its depositors.** Deposits commence drawing interest on the 1st day of each month. Drafts paid daily without notice. The deposits now remaining in bank exceed $3,000,000.

The Institution is one of the most successful and flourishing in the State.

L. S. HAPGOOD, President.

ANSON J. STONE, Treasurer.

FREDERIC H. HENSHAW, Ass't Treasurer.

ELGIN WATCHES.

The famous Railroad Watch. Quick train; adjusted to temperature; the best time-keeper in America.

18,000 beats an hour. Same train as B. W. Raymond.

MANUFACTURED BY THE

National Watch Company,

AT

ELGIN, ILLS.

Sold by the Company (without cases) at wholesale only.

FOR SALE,

IN GOLD AND SILVER CASES,

BY JEWELLERS EVERYWHERE.

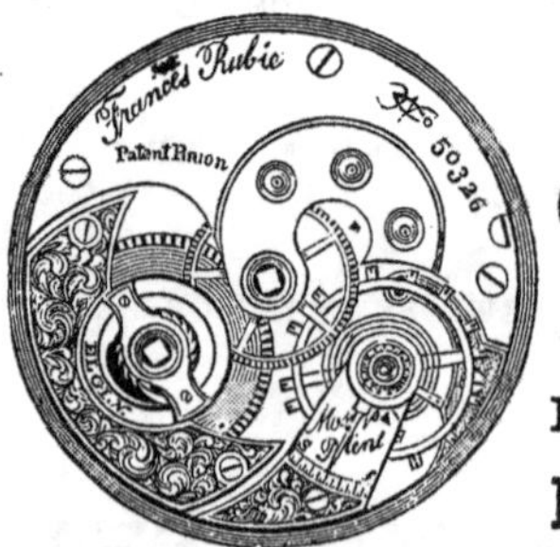

Adjusted to temperature.
The finest Lady's Watch made in this country.

Offices:

CHICAGO,
Illinois;

No. 1 Maiden Lane,
NEW YORK.

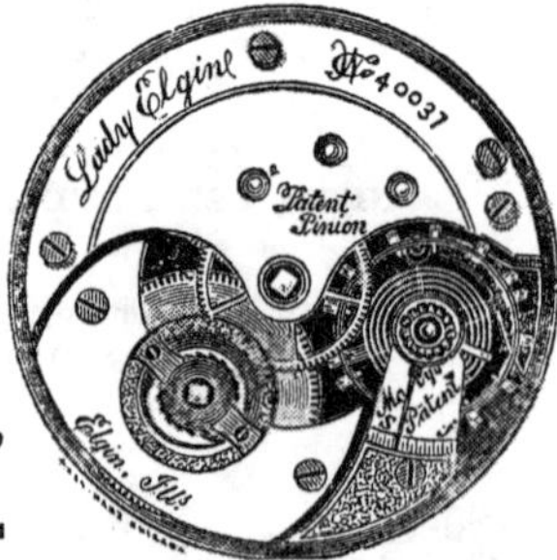

Elegant, strongly made, correct time-keepers; more of them now sold in the United States than any other American or Foreign made Lady's Watch.

TARRANT'S

EFFERVESCENT

SELTZER APERIENT.

This valuable and popular Medicine has universally received the most favorable recommendations of the **Medical Profession** and the **Public** as the MOST EFFICIENT AND AGREEABLE

SALINE APERIENT.

IT MAY BE USED WITH THE BEST EFFECT IN

Bilious and Febrile Diseases, Costiveness, Sick Headache, Nausea, Loss of Appetite, Indigestion, Acidity of the Stomach, Torpidity of the Liver, Gout, Rheumatic Affections,

AND ALL COMPLAINTS WHERE

A GENTLE AND COOLING APERIENT OR PURGATIVE

IS REQUIRED.

It is particularly adapted to the wants of Travellers by Sea and Land, Residents in Hot Climates, Persons of Sedentary habits, Invalids and Convalescents ; Captains of Vessels and Planters will find it a valuable addition to their Medicine Chests.

It is in the form of a Powder, carefully put up in bottles to keep in any climate, and merely requires water poured upon it to produce a delightful Effervescent Beverage.

Numerous testimonials, from professional and other gentlemen of the highest standing throughout the country, and its steadily increasing popularity for a series of years, strongly guarantee its efficacy and valuable character, and commend it to the favorable notice of an intelligent public.

MANUFACTURED ONLY BY THE SOLE PROPRIETORS,

STANDARD BOOKS AT RETAIL.

MESSRS. JAMES R. OSGOOD & CO.

offer at retail their own publications, in

Both Common and Fine Bindings.

THEIR LIST EMBRACES:

The only authorized American Editions of **DICKENS,** in *four* popular and elegant styles.

THE WAVERLEY NOVELS, in *two* handsome editions.

TENNYSON'S POEMS, in *twelve* different editions.

LONGFELLOW'S PROSE AND POETICAL WORKS, in *three* styles.

POETRY. — The most distinguished and popular American and British Poets, including WHITTIER, LOWELL, HOLMES, SAXE, BAYARD TAYLOR, ALDRICH, BROWNING, MATTHEW ARNOLD, BRET HARTE, HAY, H. H., LEIGH HUNT, LUCY LARCOM, STODDARD, STEDMAN, ADELAIDE PROCTER, MISS MULOCK, OWEN MEREDITH, GERALD MASSEY, MOTHERWELL, and many others.

ESSAYS — by EMERSON, WHIPPLE, HOLMES, LOWELL, THOREAU, FIELDS, C. D. WARNER, GAIL HAMILTON, DE QUINCEY, THE COUNTRY PARSON, MATTHEW ARNOLD, DR. JOHN BROWN, MRS. JAMESON, the brothers HARE, HIGGINSON, and HENRY TAYLER.

NOVELS — by HAWTHORNE, HOLMES, THACKERAY, MISS THACKERAY, MRS. STOWE, GEORGE ELIOT, EDMUND YATES, CHARLES KINGSLEY, CHARLES READE, HENRY KINGSLEY, THEODORE WINTHROP, MRS. CHILD, MRS. MARY LOWELL PUTNAM, E. STUART PHELPS, JANE AUSTEN, RICHTER, GEORGE SAND, ANNE C. SEEMULLER, HARRIET PRESCOTT SPOFFORD, MISS CUMMINS, and others.

BIOGRAPHICAL AND HISTORICAL WORKS — by PARTON, DEAN STANLEY, ARAGO, TICKNOR, FORSTER, CRABB ROBINSON, TOM HUGHES, MACKENZIE, EDMUND QUINCY, BROOKE, SMILES.

JUVENILE BOOKS — by HAWTHORNE, "CARLETON," MAYNE REID, ALICE CARY, GRACE GREENWOOD, MRS. DIAZ, TROWBRIDGE, ALDRICH, GAIL HAMILTON, STODDARD, MRS. WHITNEY, and others.

Also, the Writings of AGASSIZ, FELTON, GOETHE, HILLARD, E. E. HALE, BRET HARTE, MURRAY, CHARLES DUDLEY WARNER, H. H., MRS. LEONOWENS, NORTON, JAMES, DIO LEWIS, ROBERTSON, SWINBURNE, and numerous others.

☞ Catalogues *gratis* upon application.

MESSRS. JAMES R. OSGOOD & Co. also publish the following First-Class Periodicals:

The Atlantic Monthly,	$4.00 a year	**Every Saturday,**	$5.00 a year
Our Young Folks, . . .	2.00 "	**North American Review,**	6.00 "

☞ SEND FOR FULL PROSPECTUS.

JAMES R. OSGOOD & CO., Publishers,

124 Tremont Street, Boston.

GILMORE

TO

The Mason & Hamlin Organ Co.

GENTLEMEN: — *Having had one of your celebrated Cabinet Organs in my house for the past few years, I know not how to express my admiration of its qualities as a musical instrument. Its evenness and purity of tone its power — and, in fact, all its combinations, musical and mechanical — are wonderfully beautiful, surpassing in every respect all other Parlor Organs that have come under my notice. I should now feel myself deprived of a very great pleasure, could I not have the companionship of your magnificent instrument, and I hope the day may soon come when the rich and religious harmonies of a Mason & Hamlin Cabinet Organ will be heard in every house in the land.*

BOSTON: May 1, 1872. *Yours truly,* **P. S. GILMORE.**

"Musicians generally regard the Mason & Hamlin Organs as unequalled by any others." — THEODORE THOMAS. "The best now in use." — CHRISTINE NILSSON, ANNIE LOUISE CARY, MARIE LEON DUVAL, VICTOR CAPOUL, P. BRIGNOLI, and others. "We have not heard such pure musical tones from any others." — CLARA LOUISE KELLOGG, ADELAIDE PHILLIPS, CARL BERGMANN, and others. "Excel all instruments of the class I have ever seen." — OLE BULL. "The best instruments of the class made." — ANNA MEHLIG. "In all those qualities which constitute excellence, unrivalled." — S. B. MILLS. "Far superior to everything of its class I have seen." — L. M. GOTTSCHALK. "Superior in all respects to any I have ever seen." — EUGENE THAYER. "Excelling in quality of tone, general excellence, and durability and valu-

able improvements not found in others." — CARL ZERRAHN. "The more critically they are tested, and the more competent the judge, the more certain and high will be the meed of superiority accorded them." — JULIUS EICHBERG. "I entertain the highest opinion of Mason & Hamlin's Cabinet Organs. .... Destined to be very popular in this country." — SIR JULIUS BENEDICT, *London.* "Remarkably sweet and even-toned throughout...... I can very strongly recommend these instruments." — WILLIAM SPARK, *Mus. D., Leeds, Eng.* "Quality of tone is extremely rich and sympathetic..... Remarkable for purity of tone." — EDW. F. RIMBAULT, *London.* "Full, powerful, and of agreeable quality..... The best substitute for a pipe organ." — BRINLEY RICHARDS and RICHARD REDHEAD, *London.*

EXTRAORDINARY IMPROVEMENTS IN CABINET ORGANS.

The MASON & HAMLIN ORGAN CO., respectfully announce the introduction of improvements of much more than ordinary interest. These are

REED AND PIPE CABINET ORGANS,

invented and patented by Mr. Carl Fogelberg, a Swedish Organ builder, and the only successful combination of real pipes with reeds ever made. (*See circulars for particulars.*)

DAY'S TRANSPOSING KEY-BOARD,

Invented and patented by Mr. W. G. Day, of Baltimore, by which the performer can instantly move the Keyboard to the right or left, and so play at a higher or lower pitch. (*See particulars in circular.*)

BEING PATENTED, THESE WILL BE MADE ONLY BY THE MASON & HAMLIN CO. Also,

NEW AND ELEGANT STYLES OF DOUBLE REED CABINET ORGANS,

at very Low Prices, — $140, $132, $125 each.

Considering Capacity, Elegance, and thorough Excellence, the prices of these new styles are unprecedentedly Low.

Acknowledged to make the BEST, this Company now undertake to sell at such prices that their Organs shall be UNQUESTIONABLY CHEAPEST,

Which they certainly are enabled to do, by the possession of *Extensive Machinery* and *Unequalled Facilities for Manufacture;* and they invite attention to their present prices, which will be found as low, or even less, than the prices demanded for common and very inferior Organs.

Four-Octave Organs, $50 each Five-Octave, $100, $125, $132, $140, and upwards. Forty other styles at proportionate prices, up to $1,500 each.

New Illustrated Catalogues and Circulars, with full descriptions of new styles and improvements; also Testimonial Circular; all sent free to any address.

MASON & HAMLIN ORGAN CO.,

154 Tremont St., Boston; 596 Broadway, New York.

Cover PRINTED BY A. HOLLAND, 37 BOWKER STREET, BOSTON, MASS.

www.ingramcontent.com/pod-product-compliance
Lightning Source LLC
LaVergne TN
LVHW011237110826
845150LV00006B/1659

* 9 7 8 1 4 2 5 5 1 3 7 1 9 *